THE IDENTIFICATION AND DATING OF

Sheffield Electroplated Wares
1843–1943

E. R. MATHEAU-RAVEN

foulsham

LONDON • NEW YORK • TORONTO • SYDNEY

foulsham

The Publishing House
Bennetts Close, Cippenham
Berkshire SL1 5AP, England

ISBN 0-572-02310-3

Acknowledgements

Many thanks to Jason Dainty who provided some of
his personal time aiding my research in the Victorian
Electroplaters. To Sheffield Library's Local Studies
department and archives for their direction and clues
on the subject. To Maureen, who helped edit and
compile the text.

Typeset in Great Britain by Typesetting Solutions, Slough, Berks.
Printed by St. Edmundsbury Press, Bury St. Edmunds, Suffolk.

Author's Note

Most people who collect electroplated wares, even those who possess just one article, have sought at one time or another to learn who made the pieces – when, where and how – but they can be difficult to identify, not least because of the small amount of literature on the subject.

In recent years there has been a rapid acceleration in the prices paid for Victorian silver plated wares, in some cases surpassing similar wares made in sterling silver.

This book sets out to be a valuable reference guide to the beginner, collector, and dealer alike of Sheffield silver plated wares. With over 700 companies listed, it is the most comprehensive book on the subject to date.

Contents

Introduction

People who have a collection or just a single article of electro-plate that is marked, are often intrigued and want to know who made it, and where and when it was made.

Sheffield makers produced the majority of electroplated wares and almost without exception, stamped their marks on them. The general rule is that if it is English made and marked, it is probably Sheffield made, and if it is unmarked it is probably Birmingham made. However beware of teasets – usually only one article, the tea pot, may be marked.

This book concentrates on Sheffield makers and provides information on virtually all the 700 or so makers manufacturing between 1844 and 1943.

No one has yet written a definitive guide to the makers and marks of Victorian electroplate and one is needed, for there is a plethora of silver plated wares everywhere you look today, be it at the local junk shop, antique centres or even at car boot sales. Whilst this book is not a definitive guide, it is a step in the right direction.

A lot of modern silver plate purporting to be antique is often sold at high prices in antique shops. Conversely, truly antique pieces often trade at lower prices with the seller and purchaser none the wiser as to the authenticity of the piece.

Early pieces of electroplate, often called silver plate, are beautifully crafted and hand engraved and are important historically. If you know what you are looking for, many bargains may be had and good investments made. Just recently a pair of Martin, Hall & Co. entree dishes sold for over £450 at auction, and antique salvers are often fetching over £100 each. This strengthens the fact that Victorian silver plated wares are becoming ever more collectable and this is reflected in the prices paid for them.

For information regarding the history and background of electroplate, refer to *Victorian Electroplate* by Shirley Bury, listed in the Bibliography at the back of this book.

This book sets out be an informative reference guide to the bargain hunter, collector and dealer of antique silver plate.

Electroplate

By 1842 Elkington & Co. of Birmingham had perfected the process of silver deposition onto a preformed article. The process became known as electroplating or silver plating.

The article to be plated was placed in a solution of Potassium Cyanide with a negative pole attached to it. The positive pole was attached to a 100% pure silver sheet. A low voltage current was then passed through the solution. This allowed the silver sheet, acting as a cathode, to produce silver ions which passed into the solution and were drawn to the article, acting as an anode, adhering to its surface. The longer the process was in operation, the thicker the coating of silver.

The vat containing the solution was lined with Portland cement and had to be kept extremely clean at all times for the process to work. The quality of the finish on the resulting end product depended on this since imperfections could result from the presence of foreign bodies in the solution.

On removal from the vat the article was gently hammered over its surface to make sure that the silver coating had adhered properly. Finally the article was burnished. The most common base metals were Britannia metal and nickel silver. Other base metals used were copper, nickel, brass and British plate.

Old Sheffield Plate production quickly declined with the advent of electroplating and by the 1860s had almost ceased to be manufactured. Some Old Sheffield Platers seeking to survive converted over to electroplating and went on to prosper, the rest sadly declined and went out of business shortly after.

By the 1850s the price differential between Old Sheffield and sterling silver narrowed considerably and with rising labour costs only electroplating offered a viable economic alternative to the labour intensive Old Sheffield Plate. Its death knell sounded and its one hundred year reign was coming to an end.

An unfortunate fact was that many of the Old Sheffield Platers could not afford to scrap their existing machinery and get finance for the new electroplating process and so were eventually forced out of business.

Electroplating offered many advantages for Britannia metal smiths, primarily lower labour and material costs. Articles were either cast or spun on a lathe, and then had cast hard pewter decorative mounts applied by solder prior to plating. There was no need for expensive silver or lead filled mounts as was the case with Old Sheffield Plate. Electroplated wares used minute amounts of silver and the labour cost was less than halved.

By the 1860s the standard of living had improved for the middle classes and with it came a demand for affordable silver ware. Electroplated wares fitted this niche and thereafter became ever more popular.

Electroplated wares had stronger joints than their counterpart Old Sheffield Plate. The soft lead solder used on the latter broke easily and repairs were difficult. The majority of electroplated wares were soldered with hard solder, Britannia base metal wares being the exception, which gave a more durable and permanent joint.

Electroplated wares could be engraved prior to plating which wasn't possible on Old Sheffield Plate without putting in an expensive heavier insert. Electroplate could mimic the lines of sterling silver far better, and the variety of electroplated wares increased in scope far beyond that of Old Sheffield Plate.

Repairs to Sheffield Plate articles are very difficult. Indeed replating would greatly reduce its value. However electroplated wares could be replated for approximately a third of their original cost. The only disadvantage of electroplate was that since pure silver was used, it couldn't reach the patina of sterling silver that Old Sheffield could.

Although electroplating was not in widespread use until 1850, Britannia metal wares predating this period have often turned up silver plated. The reason for this is that after 1850 the fashion for electroplating was so popular that many owners of earlier Britannia metal wares had their articles silver plated. For example, goods marked Dixon & Smith (1804–1823) may at times crop up that have been silver plated.

Base Metals

Copper

This was a popular base metal at the start of electoplating. However as time wore on it was dropped as a base metal due to its expense. Generally, silver plated copper wares date from the early-mid Victorian period and will often have the letters EP stamped on their bases to denote electroplate. Note, however, it was still used to a lesser degree in Britain by some firms right up to the twentieth century.

The metal shows through worn areas as a pinkish or sometimes reddish brown hue.

Nickel

Pure nickel was first mined in Saxony, Germany c1830. The pure metal was used sparingly throughout the Victorian period but its alloy, nickel silver, was used more extensively since it is a good base metal.

The metal shows through worn areas as a light dull grey colour and wares usually have the letters EP stamped on their bases.

Nickel Silver

Also known as German silver and in the early days Argentine, it actually contains no silver at all. It is an alloy of copper, zinc and nickel. German silver gets its name from the fact that nickel was first mined at Saxony in Germany.

It was first used as an extra layer between copper and silver in the production of Old Sheffield Plate from about 1830.

It was soon discovered by Elkington that this alloy provided a perfect base for electroplating. It was used for this purpose from about 1842 and is still used today.

The yellow/white colour of the base metal allows easy identification on worn areas.

The words 'Hardsoldered' are occasionally seen stamped incuse on the base of the articles. Hard solder was used on electroplated wares prior to plating and is an alloy containing 50/50 nickel and silver.

Wares will have the letters EPNS or EPGS denoting electroplated nickel silver and electroplated German silver respectively. Various combinations of letters are also used i.e. EP, NS and GS.

Understandably the name German silver was dropped around the time of the First World War for patriotic reasons.

Britannia metal

There is still controversy over the discovery of this alloy but it is generally accepted that James Vickers of Sheffield pioneered the new material. It was originally called Vickers White metal and comprised 90% tin, 8% antimony and 2% copper and bismuth. Soon copper and bismuth were dropped from the formula.

It is a type of pewter that when newly processed gives the appearance of silver but over time the surfaces suffer oxidation and turn a dark grey and thus is easy to identify as a base metal.

The alloy was developed c1770 as a cheap alternative to Old Sheffield Plate and gained increasing popularity from its inception. Around 1846 it was discovered that Britannia metal could be silver plated.

Electroplating was very appealing to the Britannia metal smiths as the alloy plated very well and since their original plan was to produce a less expensive substitute to Old Sheffield Plate, electroplating was a real bonus for it brought them ever closer to their objective. Nearly all the fifty or so Britannia metal makers of Sheffield had by 1880 converted to electroplating merely by the inclusion of plating vats.

By 1870 labour costs became an increasing burden to the costs of manufactured goods and what with intense competition, it's not surprising that many Britannia metal firms started producing wares of poor quality, thin gauge and only a light coating of silver. It is these cheap electroplated wares produced during the late Victorian period that gave Britannia metal a bad reputation for being a base metal of cheap wares, even though many Sheffield companies, notably James Dixon & Sons, continued to make high quality electroplated Britannia metal wares.

The letters EPBM are usually stamped on the base of wares denoting electroplated Britannia metal.

Although this alloy was used from 1846, the abbreviation EPBM didn't come into general use until 1855. In the past goods that were badly worn were discarded as junk. However Britannia metal, being pewter, is collectable in its own right, particularly Victorian wares that are becoming ever more sought after. What can be bought now for a few pounds may well be worth a mint in years to come. So my advice is not to be put off by badly worn EPBM as you can probably buy it for very little.

British Plate

This is a form of nickel silver used by amongst others, William Hutton & Sons. The letters BP are marked on goods denoting British Plate.

Dating Clues

Approximate dating using design registration marks

Some metal wares may be dated approximately if their design was registered. Look out for a diamond shape impressed mark (1843–1883) or an impressed registration number from 1884.

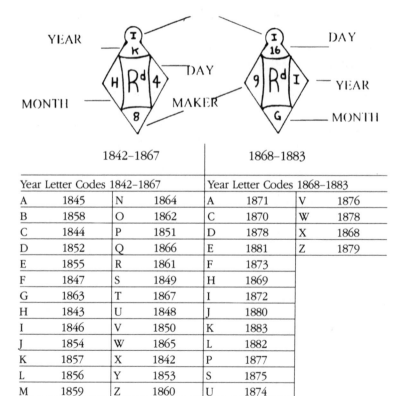

CLASS OF GOODS
IN THIS CASE
METAL

YEAR — DAY — MONTH — MAKER — DAY — YEAR — MONTH

1842–1867   1868–1883

Year Letter Codes 1842–1867				Year Letter Codes 1868–1883			
A	1845	N	1864	A	1871	V	1876
B	1858	O	1862	C	1870	W	1878
C	1844	P	1851	D	1878	X	1868
D	1852	Q	1866	E	1881	Z	1879
E	1855	R	1861	F	1873		
F	1847	S	1849	H	1869		
G	1863	T	1867	I	1872		
H	1843	U	1848	J	1880		
I	1846	V	1850	K	1883		
J	1854	W	1865	L	1882		
K	1857	X	1842	P	1877		
L	1856	Y	1853	S	1875		
M	1859	Z	1860	U	1874		

The months were the same for both series.

A	December (except 1860)	E	May	K	November and December 1860
B	October	G	February	M	June
C	January	H	April	O	January
D	September	I	July	R	August and 1-19 September 1857
				W	March

The day of the month was marked as the numbered date, i.e. the 8th was marked 8.

From 1884 registration numbers took over from the diamond registration mark:

1884	1 - 19753	1895	246975 - 268391
1885	19754 - 40479	1896	268392 - 291240
1886	40480 - 64519	1897	291241 - 311657
1887	64520 - 90482	1898	311658 - 331706
1888	90483 - 116647	1899	331707 - 351201
1889	116648 - 141272	1900-1909	351202 - 551999
1890	141273 - 163766	1910-1919	552000 - 673749
1891	163767 - 185712	1920-1929	673750 - 751159
1892	185713 - 205239	1930-1939	751160 - 837519
1893	205240 - 224719	1940-1949	837520 - 860853
1894	224720 - 246974		

Dating clues from the marks

Most Sheffield platers stamped their initials e.g. James Dixon & Sons stamped their wares J D & S. However some of the Britannia metal smiths involved with electroplating stamped the company name in full or just their surname e.g. Philip Ashberry.

Maker's Mark

Knowing who the maker is and their dates of manufacture establishes a lower and upper date of any article. e.g. Joseph Ridge was only in production during 1881–1886 (see mark 572). Knowing when changes occurred to the company title can distinguish earlier pieces from later pieces. For instance when '& Sons', 'Co.' or new partners were added, e.g. '& Sons' was added to Philip Ashberry from 1856 (see mark numbers 16–19).

Trade marks

Many companies had trademarks which could be registered from c1878. E.g. James Dixon & Sons used a trumpet and banner which was put on all their wares from 1879. Therefore pieces not having this trademark are most definitely prior to 1879.

Catalogue numbers

Generally the lower the number the earlier the piece was designed. I advise caution however, since while many companies used a sequence of three, four or five numbers, four being the most common, some didn't employ a numerical order to their classification. A few like Bradley & Blake didn't have catalogue numbers, e.g. all Joseph Ridge articles have a five digit number beginning with the number one. Obviously this company could not have produced over 10,000 different styles in only four years of production. The same goes for twentieth century marks on William Hutton & Son wares.

Addresses

A few firms stamped the initials of their address or the name of their factory site on their wares. For example, some wares by John Harrison often have the letters NW stamped on them denoting Norfolk works. See mark number 306.

Misleading Initials

Beware that sometimes an 'I' will replace 'J', for example some early James Dixon and John Harrison pieces have been seen with the stamp marks I D & S and I H & Co. respectively.

Unlisted

Only marks that have been seen by the author are listed. If you have an unlisted mark that ties in with a company shown then you can probably assume that you have found your company, bearing in mind that the majority of Victorian silver plated wares were made in Sheffield. For example a mark stamped E G & Co. would probably be by Edward Gem & Co. (1894–1900). Again caution must be used. However if you can't match up a mark it is probably Birmingham made. Refer to *Silver* by Joel Langford.

A1

This is stamped on many wares and is just a sales ploy used to imply quality.

Electroplated

This word was stamped incuse on many wares during the period 1842–1855 before the abbreviation EPNS and EPBM came into general use.

England

Never found on goods made before 1890. Commonly found on wares c1890–c1920.

Made in England

Commonly found on wares c1920 – present day.

Crown inside shield

A crown inside a shield denotes the Victorian period prior to 1897. It was used by many electroplaters particularly the Sheffield firms. The mark of course mimicked the crown used to assay silver at Sheffield. Its use stopped c1897 after the guardians at the Sheffield Assay office threatened legal action. E.g. all John Round & Son flatware having this mark was produced prior to 1897.

Plumes

Sometimes found on Victorian goods.

Initials

The majority of firms stamped their wares with their initials plus an 'S' at the end and in a sequence of 4 punches to mimic sterling silver. The marks were invariable in intaglio, that is punched in with the letters in relief. Some early marks, particularly with Britannia base metal, were stamped incuse with the company name in full.

Single number

Usually indicating the capacity in half pints. However it may also denote a variation in size of a particular style or even the workman's number.

Other letters

A single or pair of letters may indicate the workman's initials.

DWTS

This is a measure of the thickness of the silver coating. 10 DWTS was considered a good coating on electroplated wares. However 50 DWTS was a good coating on Old Sheffield Plate. This mark is not often encountered.

Dating Clues from the styles used

Engraving

Using a foot operated knurling machine could produce various patterns depending on the tool used e.g. zig zag pattern. It was quite popular until the 1870s but was very labour intensive and hence expensive which led to its eventual decline.

Foliage and floral patterns were very popular throughout the 1860–1890 period. Thick curved edges with beaded borders were also popular.

Embossing and chasing were elaborate design techniques used fairly extensively on quality wares during the 1850–1870 period.

Tea service

The styles of knobs, feet, spouts, construction and body shapes of teapots and coffee pots can be of help in dating. The information is complicated and beyond the scope of this book which is primarily designed as a reference of makers and marks. For those interested I refer you to *Pewter wares from Sheffield* by Dr J L Scott and if you can get hold of it extracts of the *Spinning Wheel Magazine* dated March, April and May 1973, also written by Dr J L Scott. These deal with Britannia metal made goods.

A brief summary of styles of teapots and coffeepots encountered

Knobs Fruit and vegetable designs   1845–c1890
Bird and animal designs   1850–c1875
Bone, ivory and mother of pearl   1870–1880

Feet   Many designs were used throughout the Victorian
period, some of which are Rim, Ball, Lion Paw,
Shell motif, Claw and Horse Foot.

Spouts Fluted base   1845–1855
Embossed leaf design   1855–1875

Motifs of curling vines and leaves were popular during the early
Victorian period.

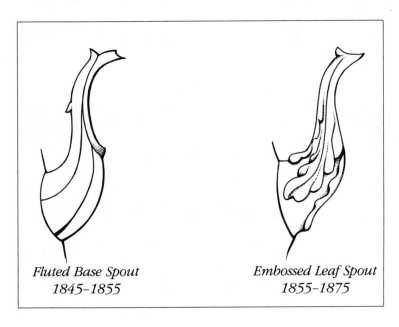

Fluted Base Spout
1845–1855

Embossed Leaf Spout
1855–1875

Body Shapes Fruit and vegetable shapes, e.g. Pear shape were popular c1850–c1860, and heavily embossed bodies c1865–c1880.

A cast article made in one piece with no seams would date from around 1870–1880.

Borders

Shell and Gadroon borders were popular throughout the Victorian period. Scroll borders became popular from c1850–1895.

5¾" dia pierced plate showing combined shell scroll and gadroon borders by Francis Howard c1885. (See mark 351 for base mark).

Beaded borders were popular from the early 1840s–c1910.

9¾" dia salver showing beaded border. Note the neo classical style engraving. By Parkin & Marshall c1885 (Mark 518).

Cutlery

Spoons, and indeed a lot of other cutlery items, followed the prevailing fashion. However, styles like the fiddle shape were predominately popular throughout the Victorian era and well into the twentieth century.

Antique spoons and forks are by far the most common objects to turn up at junk shops (particularly the fiddle shapes), often selling for relatively little. Identification of the marks allows judicious purchases to be made.

Fiddle style spoons were popular throughout the nineteenth century and into the twentieth century.

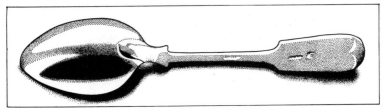

Typical fiddle shape spoon by Philip Ashberry & Sons

A brief summary of techniques and styles used throughout the Victorian period

1840s   Many electroplated wares were cast in parts and soldered together rather than produced by spinning on a lathe.

1840–1865   Antiquarianism. The Rococo revival came into being. From about 1840–1850 unembossed styles like the melon shaped teapots were popular. From about 1850 complex embossing was employed.

1840–c1880   Organic naturalism was very much in vogue and involved the copying of natural objects.

23

1849	Pierced articles, e.g. salvers, were produced no earlier than this date.
1855–1875	Adams or Louis XVI revival period brought hanging festoons, urns, rams heads, corn husks and paterae.
1855–1875	Etruscan or Graeco roman antiquities came into fashion.
1865–1910	Neo classical style came into vogue, the Adams style flowing into it with typical cast bead borders with swags, paterae and scrolling foliage. Flat chased and engraved decorations were used. Fern leaf and flower designs were very popular during this period.
1865–1890s	Japanese style.
1870–1885	Indian style.
1870–1895	Eygptian style.
	Ethnic styles were very popular from mid-late Victorian period.
1880s–c1910	Arts and crafts movement incorporating plain traditional designs usually unadorned. The period was also known as Art Nouveau. The hand beaten appearance of planished articles was popular during this period. There are many books on the market that will explain these styles in a lot more detail, some of which are listed in the select bibliography section at the back of this book.

Famous designers

Finding an electroplated article that has been attributed to a famous designer increases the value substantially. These articles were often made in limited numbers and so are rare to find.

Again, knowing what to look for increases your chance of acquiring a desirable piece.

The most famous designer would have to be Dr Christopher Dresser (1834–1904). He worked freelance and designed many pieces during the 1880s, for companies such as Hukin & Heath of Birmingham and James Dixon & Sons of Sheffield. There is usually a facsimile signature 'Chr. Dresser' as an accompaniment to other marks on the base of his creations. Examples of his works, a bonbon dish, sweetmeal bowl and toast rack have been sold recently for many hundreds of pounds at auctions.

Hugo Leven worked mainly in the Arts and Crafts movement and his works usually have the facsimile signature 'H. Leven' stamped on them.

Another famous designer was David Mellor who did a lot of work for Walker & Hall of Sheffield. A four piece tea service designed by him recently sold for £550.

What to collect

Almost anything bar a few exceptions is collectable and this can be split into two categories, namely hollow-ware and flatware.

It is much more difficult to find Victorian hollow-ware pieces these days as a great deal of it has been thrown away due to being worn out, sold for scrap or melted down during the plea for metal during World War II.

However one must beware of mass produced 'Hotel Ware' that is decidedly not collectable and was produced for the hotel and restaurant trade from the end of the nineteenth century. These articles are generally unadorned and cheap looking, sometimes even having the name of the establishment stamped on them. Hollow-ware usually takes the form of tea services, i.e. teapots, sugar bowls and cream jugs.

The firm of Walker & Hall made a great deal of hotel ware but they also made great quantities of quality hollow-ware that turn up frequently.

If you want to collect by company name undoubtedly the firm at the top of the list is James Dixon & Sons (see marks 187–

190). Their reputation is unsurpassed by any of the other Sheffield platers. Their wares are still relatively plentiful and are thus fairly easy to collect and at a modest price.

The firm originally began as Dixon & Smith in 1804 producing Britannia metal wares, becoming Dixon & Son in 1824. In 1835 two further sons were added and the company began to trade as James Dixon & Sons. James Dixon died before the firm began to electroplate in 1849. His eldest son James Willis Dixon was an accomplished salesman who spent a great deal of his time promoting their wares abroad, notably in the USA.

Up until 1878 their wares were stamped J D & S or I D & S. However two other firms with the same initials were trading at this time and so to distinguish their wares from their competitors, they registered their trumpet and banner trademark in 1879. It was used on all their Britannia metal and electroplated wares thereafter.

Up until recently the firm had always been headed by a Dixon, W. Milo Dixon being the last.

Other firms making quality hollow-ware worthy of mention are listed in alphabetical order:–

Philip Ashberry & Sons; Atkin Brothers; Thomas Bradbury & Sons; Creswick & Co.; James Deakin & Sons; Harrison Brothers & Howson; John Harrison; W W Harrison & Co.; Hawksworth Eyre & Co.; Francis Howard; William Hutton & Sons; Mappin & Webb; Martin, Hall & Co; John Nodder & Sons; Padley, Parkin & Staniforth; Parkin & Marshall; John Henry Potter; Richard Richardson; Ridge, Woodcock & Hardy; Roberts & Belk; Joseph Rodgers & Sons; John Round & Son; Shaw & Fisher; W & G Sissons; E Stacey & Sons; Walker & Hall; Henry Wilkinson & Co.

Flatware or cutlery on the other hand is far easier to collect, as huge quantities of it were produced from mid Victorian times. For this reason, masses of it turns up everywhere for as little as five pence an item. Forget forks as they are generally not collectable, but spoons on the other hand have a devout following. Antique spoons, particularly seventeenth and eighteenth century, are very rare, expensive and are beyond the means of modest collectors who have turned their attention to nineteenth century spoons thus including electroplated spoons in their collections.

Caution must be exercised as a lot of it is junk – avoid damaged or worn pieces or any pieces where the silver coating has worn away. Some of the most collectable types of spoon are the caddie spoon, jam spoon and tea spoon. Spoons in the Art Nouveau style are particularly desirable to the collector of nineteenth century spoons, but are extremely rare to find these days and are usually very expensive.

Notable quality manufacturers of flatware are listed in alphabetical order:–

George Bishop & Sons; Cooper Brothers; Charles Ellis & Co.; Issac Ellis & Sons; Henry Holdsworth; Mappin Brothers; Pinder Brothers; James Pinder & Co.; John Henry Potter; Joseph Rogers & Sons; Thomas Turner & Co.; Walker & Hall.

Some people like to collect a particular object – some of the most collectable are:- cream jugs, crumb scoops, egg cruet stands, teapots, tea caddies, and salt cellars. This buying plan makes it easy to collect wares from a variety of firms.

Yet others may only seek one or two items as period pieces perhaps to set off a Victorian dresser or table, going for wares such as a salver or maybe a tea service.

Whatever your inclination, this book will be a valuable aid in seeking out and identifying antique silver plated wares from Sheffield.

Perhaps 90 per cent of all English silver plate was produced in Sheffield. You will, from time to time come across the other makers. To this end a short list is included of the most likely that you will find, including tradenames that they used – See the Appendix.

Repairs

Removal of dents can be accomplished fairly easily on Britannia metal wares by the use of light pressure using a hard wood burnisher or even the wooden handle at the end of a hammer. Any other repairs, including replating and soldering, involve seeking professional advice although they can be done. There are a plethora of DIY works on the market to aid in the repairs of articles, one of which, *Renovating Silver, Pewter and Brass,* by

Hamish Bowie, 1980, published by Penny Pinchers would be of great use to those wishing to try. Replating is best left in the hands of firms that specialise in this field. Use of a local directory will help in locating them.

The Makers' Marks

The marks shown on the following pages are not generally shown to scale but are often enlarged to show clarity of detail. Some are obtained from articles that the author has collected and are therefore representative of the wares one may find. However variations may exist since over the years different punches may have been used.

Because the actual marks are often shown from pieces true to life, some of the detail may be lost due to wear and tear. This can well be excused by the fact that the marks shown are representative of the condition you are most likely to find them in.

The dates given are as accurate as can be and are based on company records and dates extensively researched at the local studies and archives department of Sheffield libraries.

Generally electroplaters stamped their wares with their initials using upper case letters and the ampersand (&) where necessary, in a series of four punch marks. Beware there are exceptions and caution must be exercised.

Where there are not enough letters to make up the required amount, then often unrelated letters are used and added at the end of the sequence. A very common letter used was 'S'. John Harrison sometimes used the letters 'NW' denoting Norfolk works.

Britannia metal makers sometimes stamped their wares with their full name or surname, address and the word Sheffield prior to plating. Examples of companies that did this are Philip Ashberry & Sons and John Harrison.

Different companies with the same surname may or may not be related. Connections can sometimes only be inferred by date sequencing.

Example explanation of marks

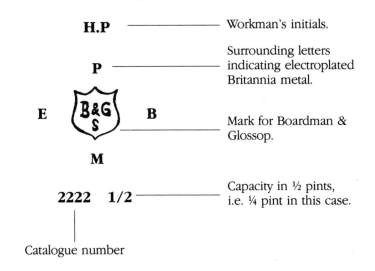

H.P ———————— Workman's initials.

P ———————— Surrounding letters indicating electroplated Britannia metal.

E **B** ———————— Mark for Boardman & Glossop.

M

2222 1/2 ———————— Capacity in ½ pints, i.e. ¼ pint in this case.

Catalogue number

General rules

1	A B C S	
	i	Where A B or C are any letters
	ii	Initials A B surname C
2	A B & C	
	i	Partners' surnames A and B and C
	ii	Brother's surname A and partner C (if B stands for brother)
3	A B & S	
	i	Inital A surname B & Son
	ii	Partners' surnames A and B and S
4	A & B S	
	i	Partners' surnames A and B
5	A B & Co	
	i	Partners A and B
	ii	Initial A Surname B

Note: Electroplated Britannia wares may have the makers full name or surname stamped on them – to this end, known Britannia metal makers who electroplated their wares will have the letter B marked in column 3 on the identification tables.

For some Trade marks of firms producing quality electroplated wares refer to pages 429–440 of *A History of Old Sheffield Plate,* by Frederick Bradbury for a full history of the makers using the following marks:

The Open Hand

1849–1875 Padley, Parkin & Staniforth.
1876–1910 William Padley & Son.

Note – This mark has been in use by various metal ware manufacturers in Sheffield since 1784.

The Pineapple

1867–1910 Hawksworth, Eyre & Co.

Note – A variation of this mark has been in use by various metal ware manufacturers in Sheffield since 1804.

The Bell

1844–1848 Roberts, Smith & Co.
1848–1858 Smith, Sissons & Co.
1858–1891 W & G Sissons.

Note – This mark was in use by Robert Cadman & Co. (Old Sheffield Platers) between 1785 and 1844.

The Sun

1865–1905 Mappin Brothers.

The firm also used this mark on their Old Sheffield Plate wares from 1850.

Note – The famous Old Sheffield Platers Mathew Boulton used this mark from 1784.

The Pair of Cross Keys

1843–1894 H Wilkinson & Co.

The firm also used this mark from 1836 on their Old Sheffield Plate.

 Note – This mark has been in use by various Sheffield metal ware firms since 1784.

The Cross Arrrows

1855–1890 Creswick & Co.
c1900–1992 William Hutton & Sons.

Note – Previously used by T & J Creswick from 1811 on Old Sheffield Plate wares.

The Eye

WITNESS

1891–c1923 Needham, Veall & Tyzack.
from mid 1920s – Taylors (stainless steel knives).

Note – Previously used on Old Sheffield Plate wares by W Ryland & Son from 1807.

Explanation of decorating techniques used on articles prior to electroplating

Chasing
Patterns marked with a hammer and punches (thus the metal is deformed and not removed as in engraving).

Engraving
Patterns worked by cutting into the surface.

Embossing
A form of relief decoration created by hammering or by the application of pressure leaving a raised pattern. This is easy to spot since a reversal of the pattern can be seen on the inside or underside of the article.

Planishing
A form of hammering leaving a hand beaten appearance. Usually the entire surface of the area was treated this way. Very popular during the Arts and Crafts movement c1880–c1910.

Explanation of Columns in the Makers' Marks Table

Column 1 Alphabetical sequence of surnames.

Column 2 Company names, addresses and dates.

Column 3 Type of wares manufactured
* = Variety of Hollow-ware
B = Britannia base metal wares
C = Cutlery
S = Sterling silver wares

Column 4 Actual electroplate manufacturing dates.

Column 5 Typical marks including trade and corporate marks.

Column 6 Location index number.

ABDEY   J Abdey, New Meadow St, 1858–1859.

ADAMS   Ebenezer Adams, 42 Cambridge St, 1885–1888; 79 Bramwell St, 1889–1891.

AGAR   M H Agar, Cook & Co., 11–13 Cumberland St and South Lane, 1897–1900.

ALLAN   James Allan, Johnson Lane, 1855–1872, started trading in 1849 producing Britannia metal wares.

ALLCARD   Allcard & Co., and Arthur Culf & Co., 34–36 Charlotte St, 1891–1893; Albert Works, Norfolk St, 1894–1900.

ALLEN   Allen & Darwin, Portland Works, 55 Arundel St, 1855–1922; 32 Victoria St, 1923–1952.

ALLISON   Allison & Londsdale, 137 Portobello St, 1884–1886.

ANDERTON   Charles Anderton, 5 Union Lane, 1860–1863; 30 Townhead St, 1864–1872; 43–47 Copper St, 1873–1886. The firm also manufactured the improved spider bicycle.

W & E Anderton, Alsop Lane, Eyre St, 1886–1891. Both sons of Charles Anderton.

Willie A Anderton, Alsop Lane, Eyre St, 1892–1900; 173 Eyre St, 1901–1904.

*	1858–1859		1
*	1885–1891		2
*	1897–1900		3
* **B**	1861–1872	JAMES ALLAN SHEFFIELD	4
* **B**	1891–1900		5
* **B** **C**	1889–1922 1923–1952	ALLEN & DARWIN JAMES ALLEN & CO.	6 7
	1923–1952	ALLENS	8
* **B**	1884–1886		9
* **B** **C** **S**	1860–1886		10
* **B** **C**	1886–1891		11
* **B** **C**	1892–1904		12

ARCHER	Henry Archer & Co., 22 Fargate, 1855–1858.
ASH	Joseph Ash, 57 Trafalgar St, 1886–1897. Became '& Son' in 1898. Joseph Ash & Son, 57 Trafalgar St, 1898–1900.
ASHBERRY	Philip Ashberry & Sons, 21 Bowling Green St, 1856–1935. Philip Ashberry began trading in 1829 making Britannia metal wares. The words 'PATENT STEEL WIRED' are found on some spoons made in the late 1850s. The words 'PATENT NON CONDUCTING HANDLE' are to be found on some wares dated 1856–75. Mark 16 is an actual mark seen on the base of a teapot. They became a Ltd Co. in 1900. Mark 18 is an actual mark seen on a spoon. The names 'SAVOY' and 'STAYBRIGHT' are seen on early twentieth century cutlery.
ASHTON	James Ashton, 12 Rock St, 1858–1859. John Ashton, Broomhill, 1858–1859.
ASMAN	Frederick C Asman & Co., 20 Cambridge St, 1905–1933; 34 Eyre St, 1934–1940. Mark 22 is an acutal mark seen on a spoon.

*	1855–1858		13
C	1886–1897		14
C	1898–1900		15
* B C	1861–1890		16
	1861–1915	 PHILIP ASHBERRY & SONS SHEFFIELD	17
	1867–1935		18
	1880–1935		19
*	1858–1859		20
*	1858–1859		21
C	1905–1940		22

ATKIN

Atkin Brothers, Truro Works, 169 Matilda St, 1853–1964.

They were formerly in the partnership of Broadhead & Atkin. Mark 23 was used only on Britannia metal wares and Mark 24 on nickel silver base metal wares, this being copied from a crumbs-coop.

Mark 25 is an actual base mark seen on a pair of sauce boats, the hand gripping plumes trade mark was also placed onto goods sold by Manoah Rhodes & Son of Bradford, and W Greenwood & Sons of Leeds and Sheffield. It has also been seen on some hotel ware accompanied with the trade name 'BARBRICOS PLATE'. They became Silver Smiths Ltd in 1923.

Mark 26 is an actual mark seen on a fork bearing the coronation mark of George VI, 1936.

Note – Catalogue numbers up to 5191 are generally pre-1900.

BADGER

William Badger, 34 Eyre St, 1894–1900.

William Badger & Co., 77 St Mary's Rd and 160 Matilda St, 1889–1897.

BAGSHAW

Bagshaw Brothers, 48 Button Lane, 1916–1942.

Frank W Bagshaw, 7 Cuthbert Rd, Langsett Rd, 1894–1900

BAGULEY

Albert Baguley, 28 Norfolk Lane, 1905–1910.

* **B** **C** **S**	From 1853		23
	From 1853		24
	From 1890		25
	20th century		26

*	1894–1900	27
* **C**	1889–1897	30

*	1916–1942	29
*	1894–1900	30

*	1905–1910	31

BAINS   William Henry Bains, 70 Trafalgar St, 1900–1904; 20 Cambridge St, 1905–1909.

BAKER   Baker & Staniforth, 22 George St, 1891–1897.

John Baker, 40 Carver St, 1847–1851.

John Baker & Co., Wheeldon Works and Phoenix Cutlery Works, Wheeldon St, 1881–1894.

John Baker & Sons, Monmouth Works, Harmer Lane, c1889. They probably only made knives.

BARBER   John Barber, 46 Eyre St, 1858–1859.

BARKER   John Barker, 38 Arundel St, 1905–1910.

John Barker, 39 Suffolk Rd, 1933–1940; 56 Howard St, 1941–1952.

BARLOW   W A Barlow, 4 Eyre Lane, 1904–1909.

BARON   George Henry Baron, Douglas Works, 23 Howard St, 1884–1891.

BARRETTA   Andrew Barretta, 36 Holly St, 1894–1897.

Wilfred Barretta, Smithfield Works, Smithfield, 1927–1930; Harbour Works, 32 Mappin St, 1931–1942.

BARTRAM   William Bartram & Co., Nimrod Works, 111 Eldon St, 1886–1887.

*	1900–1909		32
*	1891–1897		33
*	1847–1851		34
C	1881–1894		35
C	c1889		36
*	1858–1859		37
*	1905–1910		38
*	1933–1952		39
*	1904–1909		40
C	1884–1891		41
*	1894–1897		42
*	1927–1942		43
*	1886–1887		44

BATEMAN Ralph Bateman & Joseph Crookes, Bridge St, 1867–1872.

BATES John Bates & Son, 124 Rockingham St and 196-198 Solly St, 1921–1925

BATT John Batt, 18 Arundel St, 1867–1871; 20 Cambridge St, 1872–1890; 33 Broad St, 1891–1896. The firm became '& Co. Ltd' in 1896.

John Batt & Co. Ltd, 14 Sycamore St, 1896–1938. The tradename 'PARK' is known to have been used by this firm. Mark 48A is an actual mark seen on a ladle dated 1898.

William Batt, 69 Broom Spring Lane, 1861-1863. Moved and became '& Sons' in 1863.

William Batt & Sons, 7 Mulberry St, 1863–1871; 17 Sycamore St, 1872–1934.

BAUM Baum Brothers, 101 Eyre St, 1900–1903; 40 Nursery St, 1904–1925; 39 Eyre St, 1926–1930.

Maurice Baum, Albert Works, 189-191 Norfolk St, 1886–1900; Mowbray St, 1901–1904.

BAXTER George Baxter, 56 Carver St, 1884–1886.

BEAL Aaron Beal, Cliff View, Ran Moor, 1858–1859

* **B**	1867–1872		45
*	1921–1925		46
* **B** **C**	1867–1896		47
* **B** **C**	1896–1938		48
	1896–1938	**JOHN BATT & Co Ltd** **SHEFFIELD** Rd 317302	48A
* **C**	1861–1863		49
* **C**	1863–1934		50
*	1900–1930		51
*	1886–1904		52
*	1884–1886		53
*	1858–1859		54

BEARDSHAW Albert J Beardshaw & Co., 12 Mulberry St, 1863–1866; 32-35 Victoria St, 1867–1951. Was actually known to trade as Beardshaw & Co. from 1876. Mark 55 is an actual mark seen on a fork.

BEAUMONT Beaumont & Nicholson, Venture Works, Well Lane, 1907–1916.

Beaumont Brothers – see W H & J Beaumont.

Henry Beaumont, Joiner Lane, 1923–1940 formerly traded as W H & J Beaumont. Mark 57 is an actual mark seen on a fork.

John Beaumont (Forger), 108 Rockingham St, 1883–1889.

William Henry Beaumont & Co., 1 Gell St, 1881–1886.

William, Henry & Joseph Beaumont (also known as Beaumont Brothers), Nursery Lane, 1863–1864; Joiner Lane, 1865–1923. Traded as H Beaumont from 1923.

BEESTON William Beeston, Carver Lane, 1860–1861.

BELK See Roberts & Belk.

Walter Belk & Son, Kingsley Works, Young St, 1915–1931. Became 'Ltd' in 1923.

* **B** **C** **S**	1863–1951		55
*	1907–1916		56
* **C**	1923–1940		57
C	1883–1889		58
*	1881–1886		59
B **C** *	1863–1923		60
*	1860–1861		61
*	1915–1931		62

BELL   Edmund Bell, 85 Montague St, 1878–
                1881. Suceeded his father Jonathon Bell
                who had traded at this address since
                1864.

                George Bell, Belfield St, 1858–1859.

                James Bell, 17 Meadow St, 1884–1886.

BELLAMY   Bellamy & Gordon, Norfolk Lane, 1894–
                1896. Probably only made nickel silver
                wares. After the partners split, Bellamy
                formed T H Bellamy & Son, and Gordon
                formed George Gordon & Son.

                T H Bellamy & Son, Ceylon Works,
                Thomas St, 1897–1905. Probably only
                made nickel silver wares.

BENN   Joseph Benn, 50 Holly St, 1905–1910.

BENNETT   Bennett & Hibberd, Upper Hanover St,
                1865–1867; Burgess St, 1868–1872

BENTON   George & Frederick Benton, 13 Norfolk
                Lane, 1891–1915. They electroplated for
                the trade only from 1895.
                Mark 70 is an actual mark seen on a
                fork.

BERRY   H Berry, 51 Eldon St, 1858–1859.

BETTS   James R Betts, 39 Eyre St, 1928–1938.

                Thomas Betts, 1 Sarah St and 216
                Brookhill, 1915–1964; River Lane, 1965–
                1971.

C	1878–1881		63
*	1858–1859		64
*	1884–1886		65
*	1894–1896		66
*	1897–1905		67
*	1905–1910		68
*	1865–1872		69
C	1891–1894		70
*	1858–1859		71
*	1928–1938		72
*	1915–1971		73

BIGGIN

Henry Biggin & Co, Arundel Electroplate Works, Arundel St, 1881–1886. Biggin was formerly in partnership with Wolstenholme.

John Biggin (measures and handles), 12 Mulberry St, 1855–1858; 23 Sycamore St and 10 Milk St, 1859–1894. Specialised in making handles, caps and ferrules.

On Biggin's death in the 1870s the firm was managed by Exor's.

BINGHAM

Daniel Bingham & Son, 84 Trafalgar St, 1923–1934

John Willam Bingham, Trafalgar Lane, 1904–1909.

BINGLEY

Bingley,Worral & Co, Imperial Works, Holly St, 1881-1886

BIRD

Bird & Co, 85 Edward St, 1904–1910; 10 St Thomas St, 1911–1918. Became '(Sheffield) Ltd' in 1914.

BISHOP

Frederick George Bishop 87 Eyre St, 1908–1918; 29 Matilda St, 1919–1925.

George Bishop & Sons, 216 Rockingham St, 1894–1913; 158-164 Rockingham Lane, 1914–1940. Mark 82 is an actual mark seen on a spoon.

William Bishop & Sons, Spitfield Works. 22 Spitfields, 1897–1899; Joiner St, 1900–1906.

*	1881–1886		74
*	1859–1894		75
	1859–1894		76
*	1923–1934		77
*	1904–1909		78
*	1881–1886		79
*	1904–1918		80
*	1908–1925		81
C	1894–1940		82
* B	1897–1906		83

BLAKE

Thomas Henry Blake, 19 Holly Lane and 36 Holly St, 1887–1900; 19–21 Carver Lane, 1901–1911. Blake was formerly a partner in Bradley & Blake.

BLYDE

Edwin Blyde & Co., 216 Rockingham St, 1872–1878; Charleston Works, 32 Lambert St, 1879–1901; Orange St, 1902–1910.

John Blyde Ltd, Clintock Works, 24 Milton St, 1889–1952. Produced mainly table knives.

BOARDMAN

Boardman & Glossop, 54 Pond St, 1861–1871; Clarence Works, 169–171 Pond St, 1872–1927. The firm became Boardman, Glossop & Co. in 1887 and 'Ltd' in 1898. Mark 87 is an actual base mark to a bud vase and dates from c1870.

Charles Boardman, 54 Pond St, 1844–1861. He started off producing sterling silver wares but converted to electroplating in 1847 prior to teaming up with Glossop.

BOLER

Joseph Boler, 98 Wellington St, 1886–1891.

C	1887–1911	84

* **B**	1877–1910	85

C	c1940–1952	86

* **B**

H.P

B

E   B&G S   P

M

7 7 6

5

1861–1927   87

* **B** **S**	1847–1861	88

*	1886–1891	89

BOOTH   Booth & Co., 10–14, Wellington St, 1904–1910.

Booth & Thickett, 8 Hermitage St, 1858–1859. John Thickett traded on his own from 1860.

John Booth & Son, 75 Arundel St and Court 10, Brown St, 1886–1891.

BOTTOMLEY   Willis Bottomley & Son, 15 Sycamore St, 1900–1914.

BOURNE   Mrs Ann Bourne, 21 Stafford Rd, 1881–1885; 8 Sycamore St, 1886–1887.

BOWER   Joseph Henry Bower, 12 Arundel Lane, 1900–1920. According to trade directories, the firm ceased electroplating c1904.

BOWKER   Tom Beaumont Bowker, 453 Crookes Moor Rd, 1927–1931.

BRADBURY   Thomas Bradbury & Sons, 22–24 Arundel St, 1832–1916. The firm started off producing sterling silver wares and received licence to electroplate in 1853. Thomas Bradbury died in 1855. The initials in mark 98 refer to Joseph & Edward Bradbury. Bradbury was formerly in partnership with William Watson producing sterling silver ware since 1826.

*	1904–1910		90
*	1858–1859		91
*	1886–1891		92
*	1900–1914		93
*	1881–1887		94
* **B**	1900–1904		95
*	1927–1931		96
* **S**	1853–1897		97
	1863–1867		98

BRADBURY   (continued)

BRADLEY   Bradley & Blake, 62 Carver St and 98
West St, 1881–1886. Thomas Henry
Blake set up his own firm in 1887. Mark
104 is from the base of a salt cellar
dated c1884.

BRAMWELL   Bramwell & Co., Fawcett St, 1893–1896;
15 Henry St, 1897–1927. This firm
succeeded the firm of Alfred R Ecroyd.
They became 'Ltd' in 1909. Mark 105 is
a variation of the mark used by Ecroyds.
Mark 106 is an actual mark seen on a
spoon dated c1920 and is attributed to
this firm.

1867–1878		99
1878–1885		100
1858–1863		101
1889–1892		102
1892–1916		103

*
B
C   1881–1886   104

*
B   1893–1927   105

1893–1927   106

RD 680911

BRANSON   John Hugh Branson, 17 Sycamore St, 1858–1861.

BRAY   Nicholas Bray, 13 Cheney Row, 1883. He made fancy cutlery.

BREARLEY   William Brearley, 72 Edward St, 1863; 12–14 Carver St, 1864–1872. Specialised in making Epergines (centre pieces).

BRIDDON   Briddon Brothers, (Alfred & Frederick), Victoria Plate Works, 7 Eyre Lane, 1863–1896; 77 Arundel St, 1897–1904; 39–43 Suffolk Rd, 1905–1910. They became '& Co. Ltd' in 1905. Mark 110 is an actual mark seen on the base of a saucer. Mark 111 was seen on a spoon and mark 112 is taken from the 1868 trade directory.

BRIGGS   William Briggs & Co, Wentworth Plate Works, 35 Andrew St, Wickes, 1875–1922. They also traded as Briggs & Co. They became '(Sheffield) Ltd' in 1900. Mark 113 is an actual mark seen on a spoon.

BRIGHT   Joseph Bright, Norfolk St, 1858–1859.

BROADHEAD   Broadhead & Atkin, Love St, 1834–1853. Prior to forming this partnership, both were trading as Britannia metal smiths. Roger Broadhead & Henry Atkin went their separate ways in 1853, they formed

*	1858–1861		107
C	1883		108
*	1863–1872	W.B	109

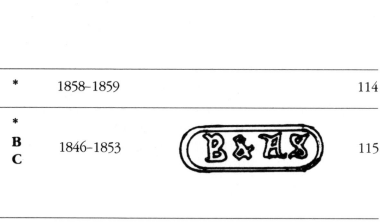

C S	1863–1910		110
	1863–1910		111
	1863–1910		112
C	1875–1922		113

*	1858–1859		114
* B C	1846–1853		115

BROADHEAD
(continued)

R Broadhead & Co., and Atkin Brothers. Mark 115 is taken from 'Pewter wares from Sheffield' by D L Scott.

R Broadhead & Co., Britannia Works, 1–3 Love St, 1853–1887; 22 George St and 4 Sycamore St, 1888–1890; Pond St, 1891–1900. Their speciality was 'Patent' Mounted Jugs.

BROOKE

Thomas Brooke, 58 Solly St, 1894–1897.

BROOKBANK

Abram Brookbank & Co., Malinda Works, Malinda St, 1884–1891.

BROWN

Brown & Lee, 229 Rockingham St, 1864–1872. They became Lee & Wigfull.

John Brown, 21 Carver St, 1894–1897. He was formerly of Parker & Brown. The firm became '& Co.' in 1897.

John Brown & Co., 21–25 Carver St, 1897–1912; 128 Eyre St, 1913–1917; 15–17 Sycamore St, 1918–1932. They became 'Electroplate Manufacturers Ltd' in 1914. Mark 121 was seen on the base of a teapot.

Joseph Brown, 227–229 Rockingham St, 1837–1864. Originally a Britannia metal maker, he began electroplating c1855. He went on to form the partnership of Brown & Lee.

* **B** **C**	1853–1900		116
*	1894–1897		117
* **B**	1884–1891		118
*	1864–1872		119
*	1894–1897		120
* **B**	1897–1932		121
* **B**	1855–1864		122

BRUMBY Brumby & Middleton, 8–12 Howard St, 1889–1892; 32 Lambert St, 1893–1897. Mark 123 is an actual mark seen on the base of a teapot.

BRUNTON George Miller Brunton 212 Brookhill, 1932–1935.

BUCKLEY William Buckley, 15 St Philips Rd, 1858–1859.

BULLAS Bullas & Co, 80 West St, c1889.

BURDEKIN John Burdekin, 7 Broom Close, Little Sheffield, 1858–1859.

 T J Burdekin, 63 Ecclesall Rd, 1858–1859

BURGESS John Burgess & Co., 7A Eyre Lane, 1921–1934.

BURNARD J Burnard & Co, Leicester Works, Leicester St, 1872–1888. Formerly James Burnard & Son.

 James Burnard & Son, 9 Suffolk St, 1863–1871. Became J Burnard & Co.

BURTON Anthony Burton, 23 Furnival St, 1900–1909.

BUSHELL H Bushell & Co., 72 Surrey St, 1910–1916.

*			
B	1889–1897	BRUMBY & MIDDLETON SHEFFIELD E.P.B.M	123
*	1932–1935		124
*	1858–1859		125
*	c1889		126
*	1858–1859		127
*	1858–1859		128
*	1921–1934		129
C	1872–1888		130
C	1863–1871		131
*	1900–1909		132
*	1910–1916		133

BUTLER   Charles Butler, 30 Washington Rd, c1872.

George Butler & Co, Trinity Works, 105 Eyre St, 1776–1925. Became 'Ltd' in 1883. They were general Sheffield Merchants and began electroplating c1872.

BUXTON   Buxton & Co, Duke Place, St Mary's Rd, 1861–1863. Formerly Buxton & Russell.

Buxton & Russell, Duke Place, St Mary's Rd, 1852–1861. Partnership between Edwin James Buxton & Samuel Russell started off making Britannia metal wares and began electroplating c1855. Russell set up his own business in 1859 and the firm became Buxton & Co.

Benjamin Buxton, 137–149 South St, C1872–1885; 163 Rockingham Rd, 1886–1890. Became Pearce & Buxton in 1891.

George Albert Buxton, 32 Eyre St, 1867–c1872. Formerly of Mammatt Buxton & Co.

CASTLETON   P Castleton, 9 Eyre St, 1858–1859.

CHAPMAN   Chapman Brothers, 25 Burgess St, 1900–1906.

CHARLES   Charles & Warner, 39 Eyre St, 1927–1930; 122 Scotland St, 1931–1942. They originally took over the old Richard Richardson site.

*	c1872		134
* C S	c1872–1925		135
* B	1861–1863		136
* B	c1855–1861		137
*	c1872–1890		138
*	1867–c1872		139
*	1858–1859		140
*	1900–1906		141
*	1927–1942		142

CLARK	(The) Alexander Co. Ltd, Welbeck Works, Hill St, 1918–1940.
	Clark & Co, 82 Backfield, 1927–1932.
CLARKE	John Clarke & Sons, 52–56 Harvest Lane, 1894–1896; Mowbray Works, Mowbray St, 1897–1923. Mark 145 is an actual base mark seen on a teapot. They became 'Ltd' in 1905.
CLEGG	Henry Clegg & Sons, Matilda Works, Matilda St, 1897–1904; 124 Fitzwilliam St, 1905–1911. Mark 146 is an actual mark seen on a spoon.
COBB	Frank Cobb & Co, 35–37 Howard St, 1905–c1940. They apparently ceased producing electroplate c1911. Mark 147 is the actual base mark seen on a bowl.
COCKER	Edmund Cocker & Co, 18 Arundel St, 1878–1881.
COLLINGS	Collings & Wallis, 23 Westfield Terrace, 1894–1900. Mark 149 is an actual mark seen on a fork.
COLLINS	Stephen G Collins, Court 7, Upper St, Philips Rd, 1878–1881.
COOPER	Cooper Brothers, 14 High St, 1850–1871; Don Plate Works, Bridge St, 1872–1885; 44 Arundel St, 1886–1964. They became '& Sons' in 1897. Mark 151 is an actual mark seen on a spoon.

C S	1918–1940		143
*	1927–1932		144
* B	1894–1923		145
C	1897–1911	H. CLEGG & SONS BEST NICKEL SILVER SHEFFIELD	146
* B	1905–c1911		147
* C	1878–1881		148
C	1894–1900	MONTANA SILVER	149
*	1878–1881		150
* B C S	1867–1964		151

COULSON

Coulson & Co, 48 Little Sheffield, 1855–1859. Samuel Coulson was formerly of Skinner, Coulson & Branson. The firm became Samuel Coulson from 1859.

Samuel Coulson, 48 Little Sheffield, 1859–1861. They became Samuel Coulson & Co.

Samuel Coulson & Co., 48 Little Sheffield 1861–1863. Probably platers to the trade only.

COWEN

James Cowen & Sons, Albion Works, Backfields. 1872–1878.

COWLISHAW

John Y Cowlishaw, 6–8 Bakers Hill, 1854–1881; Pearl Works, Arundel St, 1882–1897. Produced electroplate from 1872. His father Henry Cowlishaw had been in the cutlery trade since c1840.

CRESWICK

Creswick & Co, 10 Paternoster Row, 1855–1862; 17 Sycamore St, 1863–1871; Australian Works, 111 Arundel St, 1872–1884; 50 Charlotte St, 1885–1890. Formerly T J & N Creswick. The cross arrows trademark, mark 157 was first registered in 1811 on Old Sheffield Plate and was used throughout the firms manufacturing period. Marks 158 and 159 were probably both used only on sterling silver wares. The cross arrows trade mark was later acquired by William Hutton & Sons in 1902.

George Creswick, 80 West St, 1908–1922; 11 Carver St, 1823–1952.

*	1855–1859		152
*	1859–1861		153
*	1861–1863		154
* C	1872–1878		155
C	1872–1897		156
* C S	1855–1890		157
	1858–1863		158
	1863–1890		159
*	1908–1952		160

CRESWICK
(continued)

Thomas J Creswick, Court 1, Upper St, Philips Rd, 1878–1881.
Formerly a partner of Creswick & Co.

T J & N Creswick, 10 Paternoster Row, 1811–1855. Thomas James & Nathaniel were previously Old Sheffield platers & silversmiths. They began electroplating in 1852. The Creswick family name stretches back to 1773 in connection with silverwares. Mark 162 was first registered in 1811. Marks 163 & 164 were probably only used on sterling silver wares. The firm became Creswick & Co. in 1855.

CROOKES

R B & J Crookes, Bridge St, 1867–1872. The firm of Ralph Bateman & Joseph Crookes.

CULF

Arthur Culf, Rock Works, 34–36 Charlotte St and 185 Rockingham St, 1872–1891. '& Co.' was added in 1887. They actually started electroplating in 1878. According to *Silver* by Joel Langford, the firm used the trade name 'BLUE RIBBON ARMY'. Formed a partnership with Allcard & Co. in 1891.

CUTTS

Cutts Brothers, St Mary's Rd, 1853–1854; 90–92 Pond St, 1855–1863.

Charles Cutts, 58 St Philip's Rd, 1855–1859.

*	1878–1881		161
* S	1852–1855		162
	1852–1853		163
	1853–1855		164
* B	1867–1872		165
* B	1878–1891		166
* B C	1853–1863		167
* B	1855–1859		168

CUTTS (continued)	George Cutts, 53–59, Arundel St, 1857–1862; 29–35 Broad St, Park, 1862–1881. Became '& Sons' in 1882. Mark 169 is an actual base mark found on a teapot.
	George Cutts & Sons, Park, Britannia Metal & silver Plate Works, 29–35 Broad St, Park, 1882–1897.
	Cutts, I P Sutton & Son, 51–57 Division St, and 66 High St, 1804–1881. The firm produced a host of products including optical and mathematical equipment.
	Joseph P Cutts, 169 Matilda St, 1841–1853. Spoon maker. The site was taken over by the Atkin Brothers in 1853.
DALTON	Dalton Brothers, Albion Works, 56 Cambridge St, 1864–1878.
DAVENPORT	George Davenport, 57–59 Eyre St, 1875–1886.
	Joseph Davenport, 42 Lee Croft., 1847–1853.
DAVIS	William Davis, 254 Western Rd, Conduit Rd, 1889–1893; Reliance Place, Winter St, 1894–1897.
DAWSON	Dawson (Birmingham) Ltd, 136 West St, 1938–1952.
DEAKIN	G Deakin & Co, 107 Edward St, c1897–1909. **Note** – not to be confused with the earlier company 1849–1865 which made sterling silver wares.

GCS ⊕
2271
4

* **B** **C**	1857–1881	169
* **B** **C**	1882–1897	170
* **B**	1854–1881	171
B **C** **S**	1848–1853	172
* **C**	1864–1878	173
*	1875–1886	174
*	1847–1853	175
*	1889–1897	176
*	1938–1952	177
* **B**	1897–1909	178

DEA

DEAKIN
(continued)

James Deakin & Sons, Sidney Works, 97–101 Matilda St, 1871–1936. He was formerly of James Deakin & Co, 1868–1870. The firm ceases to be listed as an electroplater after 1898. Mark 179 is an actual mark seen on the base of a large bowl dated c1890. The lamp trademark was used throughout the period 1871–1898 The trademark 'REVLIS' is associated with the firm and seen on some cutlery.

Joseph Deakin & Sons, 114 Green Lane, 1855–1862; Spring St, 1863–1885; 51 Bridge St, 1886–1891. Mark 180 is an acutal mark seen on cutlery. The trade mark 'VENETIAN SILVER' is attributed to this firm.

DICKINSON

Charles Dickinson, 11 Carver St, 1923–1926.

E M Dickinson, Murray Works, Division St, 1889–1904; 122–124 Rockingham St, 1905–1909; 203 Arundel St, 1910–1923. Specialised in cutlery and table knives. They became 'Ltd' in 1897.

DICKSON

W L Dickson & Co. Ltd, 44 Eyre Lane, 1905–1910. Mark 185 is an actual mark seen on a spoon.

* B C S	1871–1898		179
* B C	1855–1891		180

*	1923–1926		181
C	1889–1923		182
	1889–1923		183
	1889–1923		184
C	1905–1910	D & Co Ltd	185

DIXON

Fanshaw Dixon, 89 Arundel St, 1858–1863; 49 Carver St, 1864–1877; May's Yard, Pond St, 1878–1888; 135 Lancing Rd, 1888–1894; 148 Shoreham St, 1895–1904.

James Dixon & Sons, Cornish Place, 1835–1992. James Dixon was actually in business from 1804 producing Britannia metal wares. The firm produced quality wares that are much sought after by collectors. They started producing electroplate from 1848. Early wares will often have the word 'ELECTROPLATED' stamped on the base. It appears that the firm ceased making electroplate c1935 and went into receivership in December 1992. They were subsequently sold to the Chase Montague Group & Thesco in April 1993.
Mark 187 is an actual base mark of a cream jug c1864.
Mark 188 is an actual base mark of a stand c1864.
Mark 188A was seen on cutlery and appears to be a variation of their Old Sheffield Plate mark registered in 1835.
Mark 189 is an actual base mark of a cream jug CA 1901–1925.
Mark 190 is an actual mark seen on a pair of tongs.

DOVE

Dove & Co, 100 West St, 1908–1911.

C	1858–1904	186

*
B
C
S   1848–1878

1313

$\frac{3}{4}$

187

1848–1878

190

W J

188

1848–1878

188A

A

1879–c1935

2 4 4 7

$\frac{1}{4}$

189

1890–c1935

190

*   1908–1911

191

DOVER
Frederick William Dover, 114 Rockingham St, 1905–1910.

DOXEY
Joseph Doxey, 14 Charles St, 1865–1870, and 85 Queen St, 1871–1877; Burgess St, 1878–1881.

DRABBLE
T W Drabble & Co, Orange St, 1905–1910.

DUTTON
Dutton & Benton, St Mary's Rd, 1860; 13 Norfolk Lane, 1861–1891. Mark 195 is an actual base mark seen on a bowl.

EAGLE
Eagle (The) Plate Co. Ltd, Exchange Works, Egerton St, 1921–1952.

EATON
T W Eaton & Co, 19 New Church St, 1864–1898; 220 Solly St, 1899–1911. Started electroplating in 1904.

William Charles Eaton, Melbourne Works, Sydney St, 1881–1908. Specialised in table knives.

ECROYD
Alfred R Ecroyd, Cyprus Works, Fawcett St, 1885–1893. Mark 200 was taken over from the Sheffield Plate Manufacturing Co. Ltd. The firm of Bramwell & Co. took over a variation of this mark in 1893.

EGGINGTON
William Eggington, Electroplate Works, Arundel Lane, c1876.

*	1905–1910		192
*	1865–1881		193
*	1905–1910		194
*	1860–1891	D&B E P N S 8 2 8	195
*	1921–1952		196
* B C	1904–1911	T.W. EATON & CO SHEFFIELD	197
C	1904–1911	T.E. & Cº EP NS A1	198
	1881–1908		199
* B	1885–1893	RELIABLE	200
*	c1876		201

ELLIOT Joseph Elliot & Sons, 4 Hollis Croft, 1878–1881.

ELLIOTT Richard Elliott, 151 Arundel St, 1864–1883. Went on to form the partnership of R Favell, Elliott & Co.

ELLIS Charles Ellis & Co, 39–57 Norfolk St, 1855–1900. Mark 204 is an actual mark seen on a spoon.

George Ellis, 16 John St, 1895–1896.

Issac Ellis & Sons, Portland Works, 55 Arundel St, 1878–1888; 114 Rockingham St,1889–1892; Bridge St, 1893–1899.

S M Ellis & Co, 190 Rockingham St, 1921–1939; 111 Carver St, 1940–1952. They also traded as Ellis & Co. – not to be confused with Elkington & Co. of Birmingham who usually stamped their wares with a year letter code. Mark 207 is an actual mark seen on a spoon showing the 1936 Coronation of George VI.

EVANS Frank Evans, 80 West St, 1889–1897 formerly of Jenkins & Evans.

EVISON Samuel Thomas Evison, West St Lane, 1891–1894.

EYRE Issac Eyre, Lincoln Electroplate Works, 38 Arundel St, 1884–1894. He succeeded J T Henry.

C	1878–1881		202

| *
C | 1864–1883 | | 203 |

| C | 1855–1900 | | 204 |

| * | 1895–1896 | | 205 |

| C | 1878–1899 | | 206 |

| C | 1921–1952 | | 207 |

| * | 1889–1897 | | 208 |

| * | 1891–1894 | | 209 |

| C | 1884–1894 | | 210 |

FAIRBAIRNS   William Fairbairns & Sons, 92 Arundel St, 1886–1891.

FARRER   William Farrer, 4 Eyre Lane, 1883–1885.

FAVELL   Charles Favell & Co, 111 Arundel St, 1889–1897.

R Favell, Elliot & Co, 13 Norfolk Lane, 1884–1891.

FEE   Fee & Swift, Union Works, New Edward St, 1863-1866; 21 Sycamore St, 1867–1872. John Fee previously worked for the firm of Martin, Hall & Co. for a period of some twenty years. He and Joseph Swift traded on their own from 1872.

John Fee, Norfolk Works, 171 Eyre St, 1872–1886. Formerly of Fee & Swift.

FENTON   Fenton & Anderton, 14 Norfolk Lane, 1857–1859. Frank Fenton was formerly a partner of Hukin & Fenton (1856). They probably only produced sterling silver wares. The firm became Fenton Brothers in 1859.

Fenton Brothers, 14 Norfolk Lane, 1859–1871; South Moor Works, Earl St, 1872–1910, and also 66 Porter St, 1891–1910. The Fenton name dates back to 1773 in connection with sterling silver wares and continued into the mid twentieth century. They became 'Ltd' in 1897 and ceased producing electroplate c1910.

*	1886–1891		211
C	1883–1885		212
*	1889–1897		213
*	1884–1891		214
* C	1863–1872		215
*	1872–1886		216
*	1857–1859	F & A	217
* B C S	1859–1896	F.B Rˢ	218

FENTON
(continued)

Mark 219 – The letters stand for John Frederick & Frank Fenton.
Mark 221 – The letters stand for Frank & Samuel Fenton.
Mark 222 – The letters stand for Samuel & Alfred John Fenton.
Mark 224 is an actual mark seen on a fork.

John Frederick Fenton, Orchard Rd, 1858–1859. Teamed up with his brother Frank to form Fenton Brothers.

FIDLER

Frank Fidler, 124 Randall St, 1888–1890; Advance Works, Denby St, 1891–1894. Specialised in his patent pickle spoons.

1868–1875		219
1875–1883		220
1883–1888		221
1888–1891		222
1891–1896		223
1897–c1910		224
* 1858–1859		225
C 1888–1894		226

FIELD

Alfred Field & Co., Continental Works, 23 Westfield Terrace., 1889–1913; Ark Works, Trafalgar St, 1914–1925; 17 Cambridge St & 101 Eyre St, 1926–1933. **Note** – They appeared to have traded as Alex Fraser & Co. between 1894–1900. They became 'Sheffield Ltd' in 1914. Mark 227 is an actual mark seen on a fork. Mark 228 is taken from the 1889 trade catalogue.

FISHER

Fisher & Brennan, Paternoster Works, 23-25 Paternoster Row, 1865–1872.

Harrison Fisher, Trafalgar St, 1897–1899. Became '& Co.' in 1900. Mark 230 is an actual base mark seen on a sauce boat.

Harrison Fisher & Co., Trafalgar St; Surrey Lane; Wellington St and 9 Eyre Lane; 1900–1925. The firm ceased electroplating c1925 but continued to trade thereafter. Marks 231 & 232 were both seen on spoons with 231 also on various hollow-ware items.

FLANAGAN

Flanagan & Paramore, Mays Yard, 52 Pond St, 1865–1867.

*	c1889–1933		227
	1889–1933		228
* B C	1865–1872		229
C	1897–1899		230
* C	1900–1925	H F & Co S	231
	1900–1925	MADRAS SILVER	232
* B	1865–1867		233

FLE SHEFFIELD ELECTROPLATED WARES

FLETCHER C W Fletcher & Sons Ltd, Sterling Works, 172 Bramwell Lane and 76 Arundel St, 1915–1952. Mark 234 is an actual mark seen on a fork.

John E Fletcher, 29 Eyre St,1923–1929.

William Fletcher, 2-4 Paradise St, 1872–1881.

FORD Ford & Medley Ltd, Emu Works, Eyre St, 1915–1923.

FORDHAM Fordham & Faulkner, Orchard Works, Orchard St, 1897–1899; 17-19 Cambridge St, 1900-1918.

FOSTER A H Foster & Son, 39 Suffolk Rd and Fornham St, Park, 1900–1909.

FOWLER F J Fowler, 7 Copper St, 1858–1859. Probably only made sterling silver wares.

FRASER Alex Fraser & Co, 23 Westfield Terrace, 1894–1900. **Note**– traded at the same address as Alfred Field & Co.

FREEMAN George Frederick Freeman, 87 Edward St, 1908–1916.

FURNISS A E Furniss, 12 Holly St, 1858–1862; 32 Rockingham St, 1863–1873; Eagle Place, 27 Carver St, 1874–1894; 62 Broad Lane and 13 Garden St, 1895–1910. Arthur Edward Furniss took his sons into business in 1910.

* C	1915–1952	C.W.F S EP	234
*	1923–1929		235
* C	1872–1881		236
*	1915–1923		237
*	1897–1918		238
*	1900–1909		239
*	1858–1859		240
*	c1894–1900	A F & C°	241
*	1908–1916		242
* B	1858–1910		243

FURNISS
(continued)

A E Furniss & Sons, 62 Broad Lane and 13 Garden St, 1910–1928. Became a partnership with Perchard Ltd in 1928.

A E Furniss, Son & Perchard Ltd, 62 Broad Lane and 13 Garden St, 1928–1934.

Furniss & Betts, 51 Division St, 1910–1916. James Furniss continued on his own from 1916 as did Thomas Betts.

James Furniss, 51 Division St, 1910–1923; 4 Eyre Lane; 1924–1935; 115-117 Portobello St, 1936–1944; 16A Orange St, 1945–present.
Formerly of Furniss & Betts. Became 'Ltd' in 1943.

GALLIMORE

Elizabeth Gallimore, 42 School Croft, 1860–1872. The wife of William Gallimore.

James Gallimore, 20 Kersley Rd, 1878–1881.

John Gallimore, 126-128 Eyre St, and Italian Works, 35-37 Matilda St, 1876–1896.

William Gallimore, 42 School Croft, 1840–1863. Started electroplating in 1858. Became '& Co.' in 1863.

William Gallimore & Co., 17-19 Arundel St, 1863–1891. Marks 252 and 253 were probably only used on sterling silver wares.

* B	1910–1928		244
* B	1928–1934		245
*	1910–1916		246
*	1910–present		247
C	1860–1872		248
*	1878–1881		249
* B	1876–1896		250
* B C	1858–1863		251
* B C S	1863–1891	W G	252

GALLIMORE
(continued)

William Gallimore & Sons, 15-31 Arundel St and Arundel Lane, 1891–1927. Became 'Ltd' in 1923.

GARLICK
George Garlick & Co, 24 Eyre Lane, 1865–1872.

GEM
Edward Gem & Co, 23 Westfield Terrace, 1894–1900. **Note** – Shared the same premises as Alex Fraser & Co.

GILBERT
John Gilbert, Orchard Works, Orchard Lane, 1888–1891; Sydney St, 1892–1894. Mark 257 is an actual mark seen on a fork and is very similar to their Old Sheffield Plate mark first registered in 1812.

GILPIN
Tom Gilpin Ltd, 85 Denby St, 1938–1942. Mark 258 is an actual mark seen on a spoon.

GLADWIN
Gladwin Ltd, Montgomery Works, 1921–1925; Embassy Works, 230 Rockingham St, 1926–1936. Mark 259 is an actual mark seen on a spoon dated 1935.

GLAVE
Joseph Glave, 9 Charles Lane,1888-1909.

| | 1863–1891 | | 253 |

| * B C | 1891–1927 | | 254 |

| * | 1865–1872 | | 255 |

| * | 1894–1900 | | 256 |

| * C | 1888–1894 | | 257 |

| * C | 1938–1942 | | 258 |

| * C | 1926–1935 | **GLADWIN EMBASSY PLATE** Reg No 792378 | 259 |

| * B | 1888–1909 | | 260 |

GLOSSOP George Glossop & Co. Ltd, 13 Westfield Terrace and Ellesmere Works, 59 Arundel St, 1898–1952.

GOODACRE Thomas Goodacre, 64 Holly St, 1876–1877, 154 Fitzwilliam St, 1878–1886.

GORDON Gordon & Tyas, 188 Solly St, 1923–1937; 14 Sycamore St, 1938–1952.

George Gordon & Son, Casket Works, 129 St. Mary's Rd, 1897–1927. Formerly a partner in Bellamy & Gordon.

GRAVES John George Graves, Enterprise Works, St Mary's Rd, Gell St and 169 West St, 1900–1910; Margaret St, 1911–1914. Became 'Ltd' in 1905. Both marks 265 and 266 were seen on various items of cutlery.

GRAYSON Benjamin Grayson & Son, British Works, 58 Holly St, 1872–1885; 16-18 Garden St, 1886–1893; 19 Carver Lane, 1894–1900; 99 Napier St, 1901–1910.

C	1898–1952		261
* **C**	1876–1886		262
*	1923–1952		263
*	1897–1927		264
C	1900–1914	⟨J G G ✕ S⟩	265
	1900–1914	J. G. GRAVES E P N S S	266
* **B**	1872–1910	TRADE MARK BRITISH.	267

GREAVES   Henry Greaves, 47 Chester St, 1863–1891.

John Greaves, 13 Devonshire Lane, 1891–1894.

GREEN   A & H Green, 69 Arundel St, 1894–1897.

Allan Green, 28 Cambridge St, 1894–1900.

Frederick Green, 76 Bridge St, 1891–1894. Became '& Son' in 1894.

Frederick Green & Son, 76 Bridge St, 1894–1896; London Works, 7 Eyre Lane, 1897–1900.

GREGORY   William Gregory & Sons, Westend Works, Bolsover St, 1872–1884; Otto Works, Howard St, 1885–1897.

GROVES   Richard Groves & Sons Ltd, Egerton Works, Egerton St, 1927–1942.

GUTTMAN   Issac Guttman, 26 Church St, 1872–1878.

HABBERSHAW   F Habbershaw, 48 William St, 1858–1859.

HALE   Hale Brothers, Moorfield Works, 11 Allan St, 1884–1888. Mark 278 is an actual mark seen on a fork.

*	1863–1891		268
*	1891–1894		269
*	1894–1897		270
*	1894–1900		271
*	1891–1894		272
*	1894–1900		273
C	1872–1897		274
*	1927–1942		275
*	1872–1878		276
*	1858–1859		277
* B C	1884–1888		278

HALL

Hall & Raynes, 38 Charter St, 1889–1891.

James A Hall, Meadow St, 1878–1881.

William Henry Hall, 9 Cambridge St and 111 Eldon St and 38 Matilda St, 1908–1922; 4 Holliscroft, 1923–1927. Started electroplating c1918.

HALLAMSHIRE

The Hallamshire Silversmith Co., 27-29 Norfolk Lane, 1905–1914.

HAMMOND

Hammond,Creake & Co., 63 St Mary's Rd, 1886–1935. They became 'Ltd' in 1920 and traded up to the late 1930s producing nickel silver wares. Mark 283 is an actual base mark seen on a hot water jug.

HANCOCK

Hancock Brothers & Hutchinson, 40-42 Holly St, 1894–1913. Formerly James Hancock. They were electroplaters to the trade only.

Edward E Hancock, 38 Arundel Lane and 81 Arundel St, 1883–1893.

James Hancock, 40-42 Holly St, 1858–1894. Formerly of Harris & Hancock. Electroplaters to the trade only.

William Charles Hancock, 32-36 Upper St, Philips Rd, 1875–1886.

HAND

T Hand, Crookesmoor, 1858–1859.

HAN

*	1889–1891		279
*	1878–1881		280
* **B**	1918–1927		281
* **S**	1905–1914		282
*	1886–1935	H C & Co S 5 8 5 6	283
*	1894–1913		284
C	1883–1893		285
*	1858–1894		286
* **B**	1875–1886		287
*	1858–1859		288

HANSON John Hanson Ltd, Rodgers Wheel, Norfolk St, 1922–1925.

HARDWICK James Hardwick, 39 Suffolk Rd, 1933–1940.

HARDY Hardy & Whiteley, 20 Cambridge St, 1894–1904.

Francis H Hardy, Cutts Works, Division St, 1872–1877; Clintock Works, 47 Bowden St, 1878–1890; 57 Trafalgar St, 1891–1894; 13 Devonshire Lane, 1895–1897.

James Henry Hardy, 2 Charles St and 95 Upper St, Philips Rd, 1872–1885; 33 Leicester St, 1886–1897. Mark 293 is an actual mark seen on a spoon.

HARRIS Harris & Hancock, 23 Orchard Lane, 1855–1858. Both William Harris & James Hancock set up independently in 1858.

Harris & Land, 23 Orchard Lane, 1863–1864. Formerly traded as William Harris and again from 1864. Mark 295 is an actual base mark seen on a cake basket.

G Harris, Burgess St, 1858–1859.

George Frank Harris, Milton Works, 80 Milton St, 1881–1885; Jessop St, 1886–1888.

George W Harris, 83 Arundel St, 1845–1863. Started electroplating in 1858.

*	1922–1925		289
*	1933–1940		290
*	1894–1904		291
* C	1872–1897		292
C	1872–1897		293
C	1855–1858		294
* C	1863–1864	**H & L** **E P N S**	295
*	1858–1859		296
*	1881–1888		297
* B	1858–1863		298

HARRIS
(continued)

Thomas Harris, 52 Orchard St, 1872–1878.

William Harris, 23 Orchard Lane, 1858–1863; Joiner Lane, 1864–1872. Formerly of Harris & Hancock and was known as Harris & Land during 1863–1864.

HARRISON

Harrison Brothers, Surrey St, 1849–1861. Probably only made sterling silver wares. They became Harrison Brothers and Howson in 1862.

Harrison Brothers & Howson, 45-67 Norfolk St, 1862–1899; Carver St, 1900–1909, also Shoreham Works, 70 St Mary's Rd from 1881.
James William & Henry Harrison and William Howson were cutlers to H M Queen Victoria. Their trademark, Mark 304 was taken over by Viners of Sheffield in 1923. Mark 302 is an actual mark seen on a fork.

Henry Harrison & Co, Atwell Works, Pond Hill, 1873–1881. Mark 305 is from an advert dated 1876.

*	1872–'1878		299
C	1858–1863 & 1864–1872		300
*	1849–1861		301
* C S	1862–1897		302
	1862–1909		303
	1862–1909		304
* B C S	1873–1881		305

HARRISON
(continued)

John Harrison, Norfolk Lane, 1833–1843; Norfolk Works, 116-122 Scotland St, 1843– 1865. The firm started electroplating in 1843. (John Harrison died in 1863 and the firm was managed by Executors thereafter).
He was the first to start electroplating in Sheffield and his wares are quite sought after. The firm became '& Co.' in 1866. Marks 306 and 307 both date c1860. Mark 306 is an actual base mark to a dish and mark 307 is an actual mark to an egg cruet.

John Harrison & Co, 116-122 Scotland St, 1866–1891. Formerly John Harrison, they became 'Ltd' in 1873 and were taken over by Richard Richardson in 1891. Henry Eades was the manager during the 1873–1891 period. Mark 308 was generally used on sterling silver wares.

William Harrison, 12 Porter St, 1884–1886.

William Wheatcroft Harrison, Montgomery Works, Pepper Alley, Fargate, 1857–1883; 230 Rockingham St, 1884–1911; 73 Arundel St, 1912–1918. Mark 310 is an actual mark seen on a fork.

* B C S	1843–1865	 **6 9 1**	306
	1843–1865	HARRISON NORFOLK WORKS SHEFFIELD 2746	307
* B C S	1866–1891	I H & Co	308
*	1884–1886		309
* C S	1857–1918		310

HARTLEY

Hartley, Baxter & Co. Ltd, 82 Tenter St, 1901–1904. They shared the same premises as S Hibbert & Son. The firm moved and became plain Hartley & Baxter in 1905.

Hartley & Baxter, 53 Bath St, 1905–1910; 7 Eyre Lane, 1911–1932; 40 Matilda St, 1933–1940. They shared premises with Harold Jay during 1933–1940.

William A Hartley, Central Works, 185 Rockingham St, 1894–1900. He went on to form Hartley Baxter & Co. Ltd.

HATTERSLEY

Hattersley & Falding, Snider Works, 105-109 Napier St, 1878–1890. Hattersley traded on his own from 1891.

Charles Henry Hattersley, Snider Works, 105-109 Napier St, 1891–1895; 17–19 Matilda St, 1896–1918.
Formerly a partner of Hattersley & Falding.

HAWKSLEY

George Hawksley & Co., Charlotte St Works, 30-32 Charlotte St, 1864–1865; Carver St, 1866–1946. They ceased to be listed among the electroplaters from 1867. Mark 316 is an actual mark seen on a spoon.

Robert Hawksley, Howard St, 1867–1872.

*	1901–1904		311
*	1905–1940		312
*	1894–1900		313
*	1878–1890		314
*	1891–1918		315
* B C S	1864–1867	A G H & C:S	316
*	1867–1872		317

HAWKSWORTH Hawksworth, Eyre & Co, 68 Nursery St, 1833–1868; 102 Nursery St, 1869–1878; and 122 Rockingham St, 1879–1894; 60 Rockingham St, 1895–1911. The original firm started trading in 1821 as Blagden, Hodgson & Co, producing Old Sheffield Plate. They became 'Ltd' in 1872. Mark 319 is an actual base mark seen on a salver. The letters C & J stand for Charles & John respectively. The pineapple trademark was used right up until 1911. In marks 320 & 321 the letters JKB stand for J K Bembridge who was managing director during those years. Mark 324 is an actual mark seen on a tray.

* C S	1853–1867		318
	1867–1869		319
	1873–1892		320
	1873–1892		321
	1892–1894		322
	1894–1911		323
	1867–1911		324

HAWKSWORTH
(continued)

Mark 324A is typical of marks found on twentieth century cutlery.

Hawksworth, Hand & Co, 88 Rockingham St, 1863–1864. Became Thomas Hawksworth in 1865.

Thomas Hawksworth, 88 Rockingham St, 1865–1866; 105 Devonshire St, 1867–1872; 27 Chester St, 1873–1881; 157A Devonshire St, 1882–1886; 52 Charlotte St, 1887–1894.

HAYWOOD

Joseph Haywood & Co., Glamorgan Works, Garden St, 1868–1879; Little Pond St, 1880–1900. They were general merchants. Mark 327 is an actual mark seen on a fork.

HEELEY

Heeley & Co, Neptune Works, Watery Lane and 226 Brookhill, 1894–1904. They were taken over by John Nodder & Sons in 1897. Mark 328 is an actual base mark seen on a teapot.

Heeley & Son, 67 Arundel St, 1843–1872. They took over Ratcliffe & Co. and commenced electroplating in 1867.

HENDERSON

George Henderson, 20 Orchard St, 1863–1872.

HENRY

James T Henry, Howard Lane, 1860–1870; Lincoln Works, 38 Arundel St, 1871–1884. Formerly of Stacey & Henry. Henry died in 1873 and the firm was taken over by Isaac Eyre in 1884.

* C S	20th Century	H.E.& Co CAPITAL	324A
*	1863–1864		325
*	1865–1894		326
C	1868–1900	HAYWOOD B	327
* B	1894–1904	l	328
*	1867–1872		329
*	1863–1872		330
* C	1860–1884		331

HERRIOTT   E Herriott & Sons, 51 Backfields, 1900–1904. They became F Herriott, Son & Co. in 1905.

F Herriott Son & Co, 51 Backfields, 1905–1906; 113 Arundel St, 1907–1923.

HIBBERT   S Hibbert & Son, 82 Tenter St, 1900–1909. They shared the same premises as Hartley, Baxter & Co. Mark 334 is an actual mark seen on a spoon.

HILL   Thomas Hill, 47 Norfolk St, 1881–1891.

HILLIER   F A G Hillier & Co., 57 Arundel St, 1900–1906.

HILTON   David Hilton, 85 Edward St, 1852–1858; 56-58 Upper St, Philips Rd, 1859–1861. Started electroplating in 1855.

HOBSON   Henry Hobson & Sons, 92 Queen St, 1886–1902; 23 Carver St and 28 Eyre Lane, 1903–1922; 111 Arundel St, 1923–1930.

HODGKINSON   Thomas Henry Hodgkinson, 4 Eyre Lane, 1921–1924.

HOLDEN   William Holden, 23 Arundel Lane,1927–1929.

*	1900–1904		332
*	1905–1923		333
C	1900–1909	S. HIBBERT & SON YUKON SILVER	334
* B C	1881–1891		335
*	1900–1906		336
* B	1855–1861		337
*	1886–1930		338
*	1921–1924		339
*	1927–1929		340

HOLDSWORTH — Henry Holdsworth & Sons, 83 Arundel St, 1862–1875; 172-176 Bramall Lane, 1876–1900. The Holdsworth name has been involved in Britannia metal making since 1800. Mark 341 is taken from *Pewter Wares from Sheffield* by D L Scott.

HOLLELY — Samuel Hollely, 108 Ecclesall New Rd, 1853–1855.

HOLMES — William Holmes, 154 Fitzwilliam St, 1897–1900.

HOPKINSON — H Hopkinson, 69 Arundel St, 1858–1859.

HORTON — Frederick Horton & Co., 78 Norfolk St, 1867–1872.

HOYLAND — John Hoyland, 13 Hawley Croft, 1867–1872.

HOWARD — Howard & Hawksworth, 9 Orchard Lane, 1835–1857. Started electroplating in 1853. Edwin Howard traded solely from 1857.

Edwin Howard, 9 Orchard Lane, 1857–1863; 5 Bridge St, 1870–1878.

Edwin Howard & Son, 90 Pond St, 1863–1870.

* **B** **C**	1862–1900	HOLDSWORTH & SONS	341
*	1853–1855		342
*	1897–1900		343
*	1858–1859		344
*	1867–1872		345
*	1867–1872		346
* **B** **S**	1853–1857		347
* **B**	1857–1863 & 1870–1878		348 349
* **B**	1863–1870		350

HOWARD
(continued)

Francis Howard, West End Works, 68 West St, 1870–1886; Aberdeen Works, 1 Trafalgar St and 99 Division St, 1886–1974. The firm became 'Ltd' in 1923. Mark 351 is an actual base mark of a small dish and dates from around 1885.

HOWE

William Howe, 8 Lambert St, 1861–1866; Wollen St, 1867–1872; Gatefield Works, 48 Robert St, 1873–1881.

William Howe & Co., 17 Corporation St, 1858–1861. Became plain William Howe in 1861.

HUBBARD

Hubbard & Smallwood, 29 Brittain St and Shoreham St, 1886–1887. Charles and Thomas respectively were both trading separately prior to 1886.

Arthur John Hubbard, 13 Norfolk Lane, 1892–1897.

Charles Hubbard, 29 Brittain St, 1867–1885. Partnered with Thomas Smallwood in 1886.

William Henry Hubbard, 13 Norfolk Lane, 1878–1891. His son, Arthur John, took over the business in 1892.

HULLEY

George H Hulley, 17-19 Cambridge St, 1886–1899; Ecclesall Works, 245 Rockingham St, 1900–1940.

Joseph Hulley, Fitzwilliam Lane, 1884–1886; 16 Bowden St, 1887–1897.

HUL

* C			
	1870–1974		351

* B C	1861–1881	352
* B	1858–1861	353

*	1886–1887	354
*	1892–1897	355
* C	1867–1885	356
*	1878–1891	357

*	1886–1940	358
C	1884–1897	359

HUMPHREYS   W R Humphreys & Co., Eyre St Works, 76 Eyre St, 1889–1903; Haddon Works, Denby St, 1904–1925. Became 'Ltd' in 1904.

HUNT   Harold Hunt, 82 Backfields and 9A Burgess St, 1922–1952. They shared the same premises as Ernest Ibbotson between 1931–1935.

HUNTER   Michael Hunter & Son, Talbot Works, 328 Saville St and Reed St, 1884–1925. Marks 362 & 363 were taken from *Silver* by Joel Langford. Mark 364 was taken from *Pewter Wares from Sheffield* by D L Scott.

HUTTON   William Hutton & Sons, 27 High St, 1800–1885; 140–146 West St, 1886–1929; Cornish Works, Cornish Place, 1930–present. They became 'Ltd' in 1894. Mark 365 is an actual base mark to an Entree dish which has been dated c1880. Either 6 or 8 crossed arrows on mark 366 were used from 1900. The marks were taken over from the firm of Creswick. Mark 367 is an actual mark seen on some twentieth century cutlery. The firm was taken over by James Dixon & Sons in 1930 but continues to trade under its own name up to the present day.

HYDES   Francis William Hydes, 74 Jericho St, 1876–1881; 57 Trafalgar St, 1882–1891. Mark 368 is an actual mark seen on cutlery.

*	1889–1925		360
*	1922–1952		361
* B	1884–1925	'LLAMA'	362
	1884–1925	'FUERTE'	363
	1884–1925	M. HUNTER & SONS TALBOT WORKS SHEFFIELD	364
* B C S	1843–1900	WH&SBP MP	365
	From 1900–		366
	20th Century		367
* B C	1876–1891	W F H ZS	368

IBBERSON　　George Ibberson, Central Works, 102 West St, 1894–1900. Became '& Co.' in 1901.

George Ibberson & Co., Central Works, 102 West St, 1901–1911; Violin Works, 112-116 Rockingham St, 1912–1932.

IBBETSON　　George Ibbetson, 80 Arundel Lane, 1910–1916.

L Ibbetson & Co, 48 Porter St, 1910–1916.

IBBOTSON　　Ernest Ibbotson, 82 Backfields, Moorhead, 1931–1935. He shared the same address as Harold Hunt.

G Ibbotson, 33 and 50 Holly St, 1922–1929.

JACKSON　　Jackson & Walton, Court 1, Scotland St, 1858–1866. Wilfred Jackson traded alone from 1866.

Wilfred Jackson, Hollis Croft Electroplate Works, 75-77 Hollis Croft, 1866–1911. Formerly of Jackson & Walton.

JAY　　Harold R Jay, 40 Matilda St, 1927–1939; Sykes Works, Milton St, 1940–1952. He shared the same premises as Hartley & Baxter between 1933–1939.

JEFFRIES　　Richard Neil Jeffries, 163 Upper Hanover St, 1922–1924.

*	1894–1900	369
*	1901–1932	370
*	1910–1916	371
*	1910–1916	372
*	1931–1935	373
*	1922–1929	374
* **B**	1858–1866	375
* **B**	1866–1911	376
*	1927–1952	377
*	1922–1924	378

JENKINS

Jenkins & Evans, 44 Porter St, 1886–1888. Both John and Frank, respectively, continued to trade separately from 1889.

Jenkins & Timm, 23 Orchard Lane, 1894–1900; Pensilvia Works, 188-196 Solly St, 1901–1914; 34 Eyre St, 1915–1930. Formerly both John and Herbert respectively, traded independently. They became 'Ltd' in 1915.

John Jenkins, 8 Market St, 1889–1893. Formerly of Jenkins & Evans. He went on to form the partnership of Jenkins & Timm.

JOHNSON

Christopher Johnson & Co., Western Works, 207-223 Portobello St, 1878–1952. They became 'Cutlers Ltd' in 1938. Mark 382 is an actual base mark seen on a teapot.

R M Johnson & Co, Shoreham Works, Shoreham St, 1876–1881.

JONAS

Jonas & Carnall, 95 Carver St, 1923–1928; Star Works, Arley St, 1929–1934.

JUDGE

John W Judge, 55 Trippet Lane, 1904–1907; 44 Carver St, 1908–1911.

KAY

John Kay & Son, 83 Arundel St, 1886–1888; 33 Howard St, 1889–1891.

KNIGHT

Knight Brothers, Wentworth Works, Burgess St, 1878–1881.

Henry Knight, Wentworth Works, Burgess St, 1872–1877. Became Knight Brothers in 1878.

KNI

*	1886–1888			379
*	1894–1930			380
*	1889–1893			381
C	1878–1952	(C J) (&) (C°) E P B M 1301 4		382
C	1876–1881			383
*	1923–1934			384
*	1904–1911			385
*	1886–1891			386
*	1878–1881			387
*	1872–1877			388

KNOWLES

F C Knowles & Co., Surrey Works, Granville St, 1872–1878; 149 South St, Moor, 1879–1881.

George Knowles, 29 South St, 1853–1855.

J Knowles & Son, 55-57 Burgess St, 1860–1872.

LAND

Land & Oxley, Nimrod Works,111 Eldon St, 1891–1896; 107 Trafalgar St, 1897–1900. They became T Land & Son in 1901.

T Land & Son, 107 Trafalgar St, 1901–1908; Colonial Works, Queens Rd, 1909–1977. Formerly traded as Land & Oxley. They became 'Ltd' in 1909. The firm was taken over by E H Parkin in 1952 but continued to trade under its own name until 1977.
Marks 393 and 395 are actual base marks seen on sugar bowls.

LARDER

Larder & Burgess, 144 Eyre St, 1900–1905; 38A Matilda St, 1906–1923; 156 Eyre St, 1924–1932; 10-12 Regent St, 1933–1940. Mark 396 is an actual mark seen on a spoon.

*	1872–1881		389
*	1853–1855		390
* S	1860–1872	I K & S	391
* B	1891–1900		392
* B	1901–1919	T L & S S 3 5 9 1	393
	1920–1944	TRADE CIVIC MARK E. P. B. M.	394
	1945–1977	REGISTERED CIVIC TRADEMARK 8194 E. P. B. M. MADE IN ENGLAND	395
C	1900–1940	A L & B S NS	396

LATHAM   Walter Latham, Court 4, Sarah St, 1889–
                    1892; 186 Solly St, 1893–1904. Became
                    '& Son' in 1905. Mark 397 is an actual
                    base mark seen on a bonbon stand.

                    Walter Latham & Son, 186 Solly St,
                    1905–1910.

LAYCOCK   Laycock Brothers, 17 New Church St,
                    1878–1881.

LEAPMAN   Moss Leapman, Columbia Works, West
                    St, 1897–1900.

LECLERE   Eugene Leclere, 56 Howard St, 1914–
                    1952. Upon his death in 1940 the firm
                    was managed by Executors.

LEE   Lee & Wigfall, Charlotte St, 1872–1878;
                    John St, 1879–1968. Became 'Ltd' in
                    1900. Mark 402 is taken from *Pewter
                    Wares from Sheffield* by D L Scott.
                    Mark 403 is taken from *Silver* by Joel
                    Langford. Mark 404 is an actual mark
                    seen on a fork.

                    George Lee & Co, 87 Eldon St, 1888–
                    1922; 117-119 Eldon St, 1923–1932; 82
                    Mary St, 1933–1967. Formerly traded as
                    Lee, White & Co. They were taken over
                    by Julius Isaacs & Co. in 1967. Mark 405
                    is an actual base mark seen on a teapot.

*	1889–1904	**W.L.**	397
*	1905–1910		398
*	1878–1881		399
*	1897–1900		400
*	1914–1952		401
* **B** **C**	1879–1900		402
	1879–1900	ALBION SILVER	403
	1900–1968	INSIGNIA PLATE	404
* **B**	1888–1967	G.L & Cº S SHEFFIELD ELECTROPLATE E. P. B. M	405

LEE
(continued)

James Lee & Co, 87 Eldon St,1876–1886. Became Lee, White & Co. in 1886.

Lee, White & Co., 87 Eldon St, 1886–1888. Also traded as Lee & Co. They became George Lee & Co. in 1888.

LEVESLEY

Levesley Brothers, Central Works, 102 West St, 1863–1870; Bow St and 1 Sands Paviours, 1871–1877; 74-76 Mary St, 1878–1929; 203 Arundel St, 1930–1935. Also traded as Levesley Brothers & Lloyd during 1892-1894. Marks 408 & 409 were both seen on forks.

Levesley Brothers & Lloyd – see Levesley Brothers.

LEVICK

Charles S Levick & Co., 106 Mary St, 1897–1900.

LEWIS

James Lewis & Sons, 149A London Rd, 1894–1909.

LINDLEY

Alfred Lindley, Richmond Works, 1881–1887; 99 Napier St, 1888–1890; 25-27 Eyre St, 1891–1897.

LOCKWOOD

Lockwood Brothers, 74 Arundel St, 1855–1893; Spital Hill Works, Spital Hill., 1894–1922. Started electroplating in 1884.

* **B**	1876–1886		406
* **B**	1886–1888		407
* **C** **S**	c1875–1935		408
	c1875–1935		409
* **C** **S**	1892–1894		410
*	1897–1900		411
C	1894–1909		412
* **B** **C**	1881–1897		413
C **S**	1884–1922	 PAMPA	414
	1884–1922	 MONKEY	415

LODGE   James Lodge, 100 West St, 1900–1903;
70 Trafalgar St, 1904–1911.

LONG   Long, Hawksley & Co., Hallamshire
Works, 216-220 Rockingham St, 1878–
1911. Became 'Ltd' in 1900.

LONGLEY   Longley & Hawksworth, Well Meadow St,
1894–1905.

LYDON   James Lydon & Co., 61 Orchard St,
1878–1881.

MACAULAY   Macaulay & Oxley, 48 Button Lane,
1897–1904. Became Macaulay Brothers
in 1905.

Macaulay Brothers, 48 Button Lane,
1905–1910.

MACLAURIN Maclaurin Brothers, Sidney Works, 13-20
Sidney St,1871–1925. They also traded as
James Maclaurin, Lorne Works, between
1898–1909. The firm was formerly
known as James Maclaurin & Sons.

Colin Maclaurin, 36 Brown Lane, 1925–
1929.

George Maclaurin & Son, Matilda Works,
117 Matilda St, 1881–1894. The site
formerly belonged to Wolstenholme &
Biggin. On retiring in 1894, his son,
Herbert continued with the business.

Herbert Maclaurin, Matilda Works, 1894–
1915; Sylvester St, 1916–1923.

* **B**	1900–1911		416
*	1878–1911		417
*	1894–1905		418
*	1878–1881		419
*	1897–1904		420
*	1905–1910		421
* **B** **C**	1871–1925		422
*	1925–1929		423
* **B**	1881–1894		424
* **B**	1894–1923		425

MACLAURIN (continued)	James Maclaurin & Sons, Boston Works,70 Bowden St, 1865–1870. He went on to form the partnership of Wolstenholme, Maclaurin & Co. His sons set up the firm of Maclaurin Brothers.
	Samuel Maclaurin, 227-229, Rockingham St, 1900–1916.
MAKIN	Thomas Makin, 105 Edward St, 1884–1886.
MALLENDER	George Mallender, 70 Bowden St, 1872–1886.
MAMMATT	Mammatt, Buxton & Co., Arundel Plate Works, 32 Eyre St, 1864–1867. Became George Albert Buxton & Co. from 1867. William Mammatt went back to sole trading from 1867.
	William Mammatt, 18 Arundel St, 1863–1864; 82 Division St, 1867–1881 and 121 Arundel St, 1882 – 1885. Traded as Mammatt, Buxton & Co. between 1864–1867.
	William Mammatt & Sons, Albion Plate Works, 119-121 Arundel St, 1886–1896; Portland Works, Randall St and 35-37 Townshead St, 1897–1906. Mark 432 is an actual mark seen on a fork.
	George Mammatt, 56 Jessop St, 1905–1916.

* **B**	1865–1870		426
*	1900–1916		427
C	1884–1886		428
* **C**	1872–1886		429
*	1864–1867		430
*	1863–1864 & 1867–1885		431
* **C**	1886–1906	W.M &S	432
*	1905–1916		433

MAPPIN

Mappin & Co., Royal Cutlery Works, Pond Hill, 1860–1863. Made sterling silver wares.

Mappin & Webb, Royal Cutlery Works, 179-181 Norfolk St, 1873–present, and Queens Rd from 1912. Formerly traded as Mappin, Webb & Co. They became 'Ltd' in 1900. The trade name 'PRINCES PLATE' was registered in 1887. Mark 438 is a typical twentieth century mark, this was seen on a sauce boat.

Mappin Brothers, Queens Cutlery Works, 6-10 Bakers Hill, 1850–1905. They originated in 1810 going through several name changes before settling on Mappin Brothers. They started electroplating c1865. Mark 439 is an actual mark seen on a ladle.

Mappin Webb & Co, 76 Eyre St, 1864–1872. They became Mappin & Webb in 1873.

C			
S	1860–1863		434

*	From 1873	CORPORATE MARK. **M** TRUSTWORTHY	435
C			
S			

| | From 1900 | M TRUSTWORTHY | 436 |

| | From 1887 | MAPPIN & WEBB'S PRINCE'S PLATE, R? 71552 | 437 |

| | 20th Century | MAPPIN & WEBB Lombard & SHEFFIELD MAPPIN PLATE W 20252 ⅙ PINT | 438 |

C			
S			
	1865–1905	MAPPIN BROTHERS B	439

*	1864–1872	M M & C O	440
C			
S			

MARPLES

Marples & Co., 105 Napier St, 1900–1907. They became Marples, Wingfield & Wilkins in 1908.

Thomas Marples, Continentel Works, 68 Headford St, 1855–1881. Began electroplating in 1872.

Marples Wingfield & Wilkins, Sykes Works, 148 Eyre St, 1908–1933; Portland Works, 75-77 Hill St, 1934–1953. Mark 443 is an actual base mark seen on a tankard. The firm ceased electroplating in c1940.

William Marples & Sons, unknown address. Mark 443A is an actual mark seen on a fork.

MARSHALL

William Marshall & Son, 351 Manchester Rd, 1872–1881.

MARTIN

Martin, Hall & Co., Shrewbsury Works, 47-55 Broad St Park, 1854–1934. The partners were Robert Martin & Ebenezer Hall. Became 'Ltd' in 1867.
Mark 445 is an actual mark seen on a fork and mark 446 is an actual base mark seen on a water jug.

MASON

Mason, Shepherd & Co, 37 Victoria St, 1858–1861. They became William Mason & Co.

William Mason & Co., 37 Victoria St, 1861–1863. Formerly Mason, Shepherd & Co.

* **B**	1900–1907		441
C **S**	1872–1881		442
* **B**	1908–1940	MARPLE Lᵀᴰ 1147	443
C	?		443A
C	1872–1881		444
* **B** **C** **S**	1854–1897		445
	1880–1934	M H & Co EP MARTINOID 1711 3	446
*	1858–1861		447
*	1861–1863		448

MAXFIELD — J & J Maxfield, 42 Eyre St and 169 Arundel St and 203 Arundel St, 1891–1906. They became 'Ltd' in 1904.

MAY — Mrs Emma May, 144 Eyre St, 1923–1929.

McCLORY — John McClory & Sons Ltd, Milton St, 1900–1914.

McILROY — John Percy McIlroy, 39 Bernard Lane, 1908–1911. He probably only produced nickel silver wares.

MEDLEY — Tom Medley, 38 Brown Lane, 1897–1900.

MEESON — Meeson & Co, Cambridge St, 1892–1897.

Meeson & Green, Orchard Works, Orchard Lane, 1872–1885. They became James Meeson & Son from 1882.

Meeson & Millington, Orchard Works, Orchard Lane, 1889–1891. Formerly traded as James Meeson & Son. They became Meeson & Co. in 1892.

James Meeson & Son, Orchard Works, Orchard Lane, 1882–1888. They became Meeson & Millington in 1889.

MEMMOTT — Memmott Brothers, 20 Cambridge St., 1894–c1952.

Walter G Memmott, 22 Charles St, 1872–1881; 88 Backfields, 1882–1884.

*	1891–1906	449
*	1923–1929	450
*	1900–1914	451
*	1908–1911	452
*	1897–1900	453
*	1892–1897	454
* **B** **C**	1872–1885	455
* **C**	1889–1891	456
* **C**	1882–1888	457
*	1894–c1952	458
C	1872–1884	459

METHLEY Methley & Wilson, 94 Wellington St, 1863–1864. S Wilson traded on his own from 1865.

METZ Paul Metz, 122 Rockingham St, c1863.

MILLS Frank Mills & Co., 63 Division St, 1894–1906. Mark 462 is an actual base mark seen on a salt cellar.

MILLWARD A Millward, 32-34 Eyre St, 1858–1864. He was an electroplater to the trade only, becoming A & W Millward in 1865.

A & W Millward, 39 Eyre St, 1865–1872. Started electroplating in 1868.

MILNS Arthur Milns & Co., 74-89 Arundel St,1900–1928.

MORTON Henry Morton & Co,, London Works, Bridge St, 1872–1877; Portland Works, 222 West St, 1878–1900. They specialised in candlesticks.

William Morton, 82 Stafford St Park, 1897–1900.

MOSLEY R F Mosley & Co. Ltd, Portland Works, Randall St,1900-1911. Mark 468 is an actual mark seen on a spoon.

NEEDHAM Arnold Needham & Co, 95 Eldon St, 1905–1911.

* **B**	1863–1864		460
*	c1863		461
* **B**	1894–1906	FRANK MILLS & Co	462
*	1858–1864		463
*	1868–1872		464
* **B**	1900-1928		465
*	1872–1900		466
*	1897–1900		467
C	1900–1911		468
*	1905–1911		469

NEEDHAM
(continued)

J Needham (Caps, Ferrules, & Co.), Jehn Lane, 1848–1866; 53 Arundel St, 1867–1872; 69 Arundel St, 1872–1891. He started electroplating in 1867.

Needham, Veall & Tyzack, Eye Witness Works, Milton St, 1889–1925; Nimrod Works, Eldon St, 1889–1905; Glamorgan Works, Pond St and Pyramid Works, Reed St and Ceylon Works, Thomas St, 1905–1925. They became 'Ltd' in 1897. Tyzack was formerly of Tyzack, Vincent & Co. The trademark was taken over by Taylors of Sheffield in the 1920s. They specialised in blades and scissors.
The trade mark BURMA SILVER is sometimes seen on cutlery.

NEILL

Stanley Neill & Co., 198 West St, 1904–1909.

NEWELL

E Newell & Co., 58 Holly St, 1900–1904; 97-99 Edward St, 1905–1916; Court 2, Burgess St,1917–1926; 226 Solly St, 1927–1940; 124 Scotland St, 1941–1952.

NICHOLSON

Nicholson & White, North St Works, 53 North St, 1853–1855. They became Nicholson, White & Co. in 1856.

Nicholson White & Co., 53 North St, 1856–1858.

NIXON

Charles Edward Nixon, Wolfram's Works, 185 Rockingham St, 1881–1885; 226 Brookhill and 103 Napier St, 1886–1897.

* S	1867–1891		470
* C		TRADE MARK. **WITNESS**	
	1889–1925		471
	1889–1925		471A
*	1904–1909		472
*	1900–1952		473
* B	1853–1855		474
* B	1856–1858		475
*	1881–1897		476

NODDER

John Nodder & Sons, 188 Rockingham St, 1863–1864; Taranaki Works, Dunfields., 1864–1868; Taranaki Works, 138-140 New Edward St, 1868–1889; 226 Brookhill, 1889–1904. They became 'Ltd' in 1897 and acquired the firm of Heeley & Co in 1897. Mark 477 is an actual base mark to a teapot c1875. Marks 479 and 480 are usually seen on cutlery.

NOWILL

John Nowill & Sons, Nowill's Cutlery & Plate Works, 115-135 Scotland St, 1864–1949; Trimils Works, 87 London Rd, 1950–1965. The became 'Ltd' in 1928. According to *Silver* by Joel Langford the firm used the crossed keys trademark but it is not clear whether they acquired this from Henry Wilkinson & Co. in 1894. Mark 481 is an actual mark seen on cutlery. Mark 483 is attributed to this firm and was seen on the base of a sugar bowl.
The Nowill name has been associated with silver ware as far back as 1783 in Sheffield.

*
B
C
S 1863–1904

5

JOHN NODDER
& SONS
SHEFFIELD

2 3 5 2

477

c1890–1904

TRADE MARK.

478

1897–1904 OSMIUM SILVER 479

1897–1904 NODDERS SILVER 480

*
B
C 1864–1897 481

1898–1927 482

1928–1965   483

NUTT
William R Nutt, Wentworth Works, 23 Burgess St, 1878–1891. Became '& Co' in 1892.

W R Nutt & Co., 39-43 Suffolk Rd, 1892–1904.

OATES
Oates & Hudson, Cutts Works, Yard, 41 Division St, 1867–1872.

OLDALE
Thomas Oldale, 56 Carver St, 1927–1940.

OLDHAM
Oldham & Sewell, School of Arts Works, 53 Arundel St, 1863–1872; 69 Arundel St, 1873–1877. James Oldham traded solely from 1877.

James Oldham, School of Arts Works, 69 Arundel St, 1877–1895. Became '& Co.' in 1896.

James Oldham & Co, Surrey Lane, 1896–1900.

ORFORD
Orford & Co., Surrey Plate Works, Surrey Lane, 1927–1935.

OSBORNE
William Osborne, 82 Backfields, 1905–1908. Became '& Co.' in 1909.

Osborne & Co, 82 Backfields, 1909–1911; 122 Rockingham St,1912–1916; 207 Rockingham St, 1917–1940, They became 'Sheffield Ltd' in 1927.

*	1878–1891	484
* **B**	1892–1904	485
* **B**	1867–1872	486
*	1927–1940	487
* **b**	1863–1877	488
* **B**	1877–1895	489
* **B**	1896–1900	490
* **B**	1927–1935	491
* **B**	1905–1908	492
* **B**	1909–1940	493

OTLEY   Thomas Otley, Lambert St, 1861–1864; Meadow Works, 33 New Meadow St, 1865–1872. Became '& Sons' in 1872.

Thomas Otley & Sons, Meadow Works, 33 New Meadow St, 1872–1911. They became 'Cutlery Ltd' in 1900.

William Otley & Co., 69 Henry St, 1891–1894.

OWEN   Owen & Bottomley, 17 Figtree Lane, 1878–1883. Became Lewis Thomas Owen in 1884.

Owen & Priestley, Tudor Place, Tudor St, 1878–1881.

Owen & Wild, 34-36 Holly St, 1888–1904.

Owen Brothers, 12 Bakers Hill, 1878–1888. Also traded as James Owen.

Charles Owen, 92 Wellington St, 1853–1854; Wellington Works, 130 West St, 1855–1860; 3-7 Eldon St, 1861–1863. Also 111 Arundel St, 1881–1884; Moorhead Works, 48 Button Lane, 1885–1893; 92 Arundel St, 1894–1896. Became '& Co.' in 1863.

Charles Owen & Co, 3-7 Eldon St, 1863–1871; 12 Bakers Hill, 1872–1878. Formerly Charles Owen, went on to trade as Owen Brothers from 1878.

* B C	1861–1872	494
* B C	1872–1911	495
* B	1891–1894	496
*	1878–1883	497
*	1878–1881	498
*	1888–1904	499
* B C	1878–1888	500
* B	1853–1863	501
	&	
	1881–1896	502
* B	1863–1878	503

OWEN
(continued)

Denison Owen, Victoria Mills, Corporation St, 1878–1881; Victoria Works, 54 Allen St, 1882–1886.

James Owen – *see* Owen Brothers.

Lewis Thomas Owen, 17 Figtree Lane, 1884–1885. Formerly traded as Owen & Bottomley.

Robert Owen, 58 Allen St, c1876.

PADLEY

Padley, Parkin & Co. – *see* Padley, Parkin & Staniforth.

Padley,Parkin & Staniforth, 1 Watson Walk, Angel St,1846–1875. Formerly traded as Padley, Parkin & Co. making Old Sheffield Plate and sterling silver wares. The palm of hand trademark was acquired from J Watson & Son in 1849. They also traded as Padley, Staniforth & Co. William Padley set up a new firm trading with his son in 1876. Mark 509 is an actual base mark of a dish dated c1872.

Padley Staniforth & Co. – *see* Padley, Parkin & Staniforth.

William Padley & Son, 57 Burgess St, 1876–1882; 88 Surrey St, 1883–1890; 8-12 Howard St, 1891–1903; Meadow St, 1904–1911. Formerly of Padley, Parkin & Staniforth. They became 'Ltd' in 1900. Mark 511 is an actual base mark seen on a condiment stand.

* **B**	1878–1881	504
* **B** **C**	1883–1886	505
*	1884–1885	506
* **B**	c1876	507

* **S**	1849–1875	508
* **S**		
	1849–1875	509
* **S**	1849–1875	510
*		
	1876–1911	511

PAGE

Owen Page, 1858–1859; 14 Upper St, Philips Rd, 1858–1859.

PAGET

Paget & Senior Ltd, 145 Eldon St, 1918–1925. Senior partnered with Farquharson in 1926.

PARKER

Parker & Brown, Progress Works, 38 Garden St, 1875–1894. John Brown set up his own firm in 1894.

Joseph Parker, Pool Works, 3 Burgess St, 1858–1863; 69 Arundel St, 1863–1872. Became '& Sons' in 1872.

Joseph Parker & Sons, Alexandra Works, 58-60 Trinity St, 1872–1935.

PARKIN

Parkin & Co. – *see* E H Parkin & Co.

Parkin & Marshall, Telegraph Works, 23 Furnival St, 1770–1892; Sylvester St, 1893–1914; Milton St, 1915–1924. Marshall died in 1852 & Parkin in 1873, the firm being succeeded by Parkin's sons, William & Bernard from 1873. They started electroplating in 1861. Mark 518 is an actual base mark to a salver.

*	1858–1859		512
*	1918–1925		513
* C	1875–1894		514
* B C	1858–1872		515
* B C	1872–1935	J P & S	516
* B	1919–Present		517
* B C S	1861–1924	P & M S 3 8 7 4	518
	1861–1924	XL ALL	519
	1874–1924		520
	1882–1924	SHARP EDGE	521

PARKIN
(continued)

E H Parkin & Co., 212 Brookhill, 1919–1928; 122 Scotland St, 1929–present. They became 'Ltd' in 1940 and 'Silversmiths Ltd' in 1977. Also traded as Parkin & Co. Mark 522 is an actual base mark seen on a teapot.

George Parkin, 121 Ecclesall St, 1853–1855.

Richard Parkin, 30 Pond Hill, 1836–1853. Formerly of Thomas & Richard Parkin, he is not thought to have produced electroplate. Became '& Son' in 1853.

Richard Parkin & Son, 30 Pond Hill, 1853–1872. Started electroplating in 1857.

Thomas Parkin, 15 Sycamore St, 1836–1872. Formerly of Thomas & Richard Parkin. Began electroplating in 1855.

PASHLEY

Pashley & Tyas, Dunn St, 1863–1864.

PASLEY

Richard F Pasley, Anchor Works, Rockingham St, 1878–1884; Mary St, 1885–1891.

PEACE

Peace, Sons & Varley Ltd, 126 Corporation St, 1921–1925.

PEARCE

Pearce & Buxton, Naga Works, Eyre Lane, 1891–1893. Benjamin Buxton formerly traded under his own name. H R Pearce traded with his son from 1894.

*
B

1919–Present ⟦E⟧ ⟦P⟧ ⟦E H P⟧ ⟦B⟧ ⟦M⟧   522
          ⟦& Cº S⟧

           5 2 5 6

*   1853–1855   523

B   1836–1853   524

*
B   1857–1872   525

*
B   1855–1872   526

---

*   1863–1864   527

---

*   1878–1891   528

---

*   1921– 1925   529

---

*   1891–1893   530

PEARCE
(continued)

H R Pearce & Son, 156 Rockingham Lane, 1894–1896; 333 London Rd, 1897–1900.

John Pearce & Co, 28 Eyre Lane, 1904–1922.

PEERLESS

Peerless Plate Manufacturing Co. Ltd, 55 Brown St, 1923–1934.

PETFIELD

Frank Petfield, 89 Arundel St, 1910–1925.

Petfield, Harrison & Wilson, Havelock Works, Walker St, Wickes, 1876–1877. Jackson Petfield traded alone from 1878.

Jackson Petfield, Havelock Works, Walker St, Wickes, 1878–1881.

PINDER

Pinder Brothers, 142 Rockingham St, 1885–1892; 48 Garden St, 1892–1940; Sheaf Plate Works, Arundel St, 1940–1950; 87 London Rd, 1950–present. They became 'Ltd' in 1923. The trade name 'CONSORT'is associated with this firm. Mark 537 is an actual mark seen on a tea spoon dated c1950.

Charles Edward Pinder, 2 Fitzwilliam Lane, 1881–1885.

James Pinder & Co., Colonial Plate Works, 12-14 Carver St, 1877–1894. Marks 539 and 540 were both seen on a various items of cutlery.

* C	1894–1900		531
*	1904–1922		532
*	1923–1934		533
*	1910–1925		534
* B	1876–1877		535
* B	1878–1881		536
C	1923–Present	P.BROS.(S) LTD "CONSORT"	537
*	1881–1885		538
C	1877–1894		539
	1877–1894	J.P PARAGON METAL &Cº	540

PINDER
(continued)

John T Pinder, Court 2, Headford St, 1877–1881.

PLATING

The Plating Co. Ltd, 239 Solly St and Wheeldon St, 1881–1934. They plated for the trade only from 1894. The manager during the early years was W D Bocking.

POTTER

John Henry Potter, 124 Rockingham St, 1884–1893; Rockingham Works, 65-71 Division St, 1893–1940. They became '& Sons Ltd' in 1922. Mark 543 is an actual mark seen on a fork. Mark 544 is an actual base mark seen on a tankard. Mark 545 is an actual base mark to a cream jug. Mark 546 is also from a cream jug. Usually only the word 'SILVA' is used from the trademark. Mark 547 is often encountered on cutlery. Mark 548 is an actual mark seen on cutlery.

The trademark DIUM is sometimes encountered on 20th Century cutlery.

*	1877–1881		541
*	1881–1894		542
* B C	1884–1890		543
	1884–1921	J. H. P.	544
	1884–1921	SUPERIOR PLATE	545
	1884–1921	POTTER SHEFFIELD A1	546
	1884–1940	 SILVA	547
	20th Century		547a
	1922–1940	J H P & S	548

PRICE   Joseph Price, 66 Wicker Lane, 1862–
1866; Turbot Works, Hermitage St, 1867–
1894. Also traded as '& Sons' during
1889–1891.

PRIESTLEY   Priestley & Co. – *see* Arthur Priestley &
Co.

Arthur Priestley & Co., 4 Carver Lane,
1891–1900. Also traded as Priestley &
Co. during 1895–1900.

PRYOR   Prior & Tyzack, 80 Division St, 1863–
1867. Formerly traded as Pryor, Tyzack &
Co. Edward Tyzack continued to trade
from this address after 1867.

Pryor, Tyzack & Co., 175 Granville St,
1860–1861; 80 Division St, 1862–1863.
Beame Pryor & Tyzack in 1863.

RAMSDEN   Benjamin W Ramsden, Livingstone
Works, 54 Holly St and 124 Rockingham
St, 1872–1897. Mark 554 is their actual
trademark.

RATCLIFFE   Ratcliffe & Co., 67 Arundel St, 1859–
1867. They were bought out by Heeley
& Son in 1867.

John & Charles Ratcliffe & Co., 67
Arundel St, 1852-1859. Became Ratcliffe
& Co. in 1859.

Rowland Ratcliffe & Sons, London
Works, Bridge St, 1884–1886.

C	1862–1894		549
* **C**	1895–1900		550
* **C**	1891–1900		551
*	1863–1867		552
*	1860–1863		553
* **C**	1872–1897		554
*	1859–1867		555
*	1852–1859		556
*	1884–1886		557

RAWSON

Rawson Brothers, Globe Cutlery Works, 19-27 Carver St, 1878–1906.

RAYNES

Joseph Raynes, 13 Norfolk Lane, 1894–1897.

RETCHFORD

Samuel Retchford, 29 Norfolk Lane, 1858–1860; 8 Heritage St, 1861–1863.

REYNOLDS

Frederick Reynolds Ltd, 116-118 Gell St, 1931–1940. They became '(1936) Ltd' in 1936.

RHODES

Rhodes & Beardshaw, 12 Mulberry St, 1861–1863. Albert J Beardshaw continued to trade from this address after 1863. Jehoida Alsop Rhodes moved to Howard St. They formerly traded as Rhodes Brothers.

Rhodes Brothers, 12 Mulberry St, 1853–1861, Became Rhodes & Beardshaw in 1861. Also Exchange Works, 80 West St, 1877–1881.

F Rhodes & Sons, 100 West St, 1908–1911.

Jehoida Alsop Rhodes, Britain Works, 53 Howard St, 1863–1878. Formerly Rhodes & Beardshaw. They became J A Rhodes & Barber in 1878.

J A Rhodes & Barber, Britain Works, 53 Howard St, 1878–1886.

William H Rhodes, Rockingham Lane, 1877–1881.

C	1878–1906	558
*	1894–1897	559
*	1858–1863	560
*	1931–1940	561
*	1861–1863	562
*	1853–1861	563
*	1877–1881	564
*	1908–1911	565
*	1863–1878	566

*	1878–1886	567
*	1877–1881	568

RICHARDS   Mrs A Richards, Smiths Wheel, Sydney St,
                 1878–1881.

RICHARDSON   Richardson & Binney Ltd,16-20 Bowdon
                 St, 1927–1940; 117 Eldon St, 1941–1952.

                 Richard Richardson, Cornwall Works,
                 30 Pond Hill, 1796–1883; 161-167
                 Norfolk St, 1883–1890; 116-122 Scotland
                 St, 1891–1924. Started electroplating in
                 1873. Mark 571 is the actual base mark
                 of an urn dated c1890. They acquired
                 the firm of John Harrison & Co. Ltd in
                 1891 and became 'Ltd' in 1910. Charles
                 & Warner took over the site in 1924.

RIDGE   Joseph Ridge & Co., Lion Works, 47 Eyre
                 Lane, 1881–1886. Previously a partner of
                 Ridge, Woodcock & Hardy, Ridge had
                 contacts in Birmingham and may have
                 traded there until 1890. However, it is
                 known that he was manager of John
                 Round & Sons between 1890–1915.
                 Mark 572 is the actual base mark to a
                 slop bowl dated c1884.

                 Ridge Woodcock & Hardy, Jepsons
                 Wheel, Jessop St, 1872–1875; Eldon
                 Place, 143-145 Eldon St, 1876–1881.
                 Joseph Ridge left the partnership to
                 trade on his own from 1881. Woodcock
                 & Hardy continued to trade using the
                 same trademark.

*	1878–1881		569

*	1927–1952		570

*
B
C
S 1873–1924  571

*
B

1881–1886 572

*
B 1872–1881 573

ROBERTS

Roberts & Belk, Furnival Works, 38 Furnival St, 1864 – present. Formerly traded as Roberts & Briggs. In mark 576 the letters stand for Samuel Roberts & Charles Belk. On Roberts retirement in 1879, a new partner was taken on. The firm became 'Ltd' in 1901. According to *Silver* by Joel Langford, the trade name 'SYLFERET' was also used. Mark 579 is the company trademark first seen in trade catalogues in 1895. It appears from trade catalogues that the company ceased electroplating c1920.

Roberts & Briggs, Furnival Works, 38 Furnival St, 1859–1863. The firm had its roots back in 1809 trading as Furniss, Pole & Turner, the Old Sheffield Platers becoming W Briggs c1823. The firm became Roberts & Belk in 1864.

Roberts & Co., Shoreham Works, Shoreham St, 1858–1872. Formerly traded as Roberts & Hall, they went on to become Roberts & Timm.

* **B** **C** **S**	1864–1867	R & B	574
	1864–1867	R & B	575
	1867–1879	S R C B	576
	1879–1892	C B E P	577
	1892–c1920	R & B	578
	1895–c1920	TRADE MARK.	579
* **B** **C** **S**	1859–1863	R & B	580
* **B**	1858–1872		581

ROBERTS
(continued)

Roberts & Hall, 51 Broad St Park, 1847–1858. They became Roberts & Co. in 1858.

Roberts & Manico, 41 Eyre St, 1894–1904. William Roberts formerly traded on his own.

Roberts & Slater, 38 Furnival St, 1845–1859. They became Roberts & Briggs in 1860.

Roberts & Timms, 23 Orchard Lane, 1873–1888. Formerly traded as Roberts & Co. Both William Roberts & Herbert Timm traded separately from 1888.

Roberts, Booth & Co., 12-14 Wellington St, 1908–1911.

Roberts Dore & Hall (Sheffield) Ltd, 1916–1923. Marks 587 and 588 are actual base marks seen on a salver and tankard respectively. The firm continued to trade from London after 1923.

Roberts, Smith & Co., Eyre St, 1828–1848. They started electroplating in 1844. Formerly Old Sheffield Platers. They became Smith, Sissons & Co. in 1848.

William Roberts, 4 Carver Lane, 1889–1893. Formerly a partner in Roberts & Timm, went on to form Roberts & Manico in 1894.

*	1847–1858		582
*	1894–1904		583
* S	c1855–1859		584
* S	1873–1888		585
*	1908–1911		586
* B	1916–1919	E P R&D S.L N S	587
	1920–1923	E P RAND R&D LTD N S	588
*	1844–1848	(bell mark)	589
*	1889–1893		590

ROBINSON   Robinson & Oates, 47 Eyre Lane, 1897–1901.

Edward Robinson & Co., Eyre Street Works, 54-60 Eyre St, 1863–1875; 32 Pinstone St, 1876–1879; 8 Westfield Terrace, 1880–1886. Mark 592 is an actual mark seen on a spoon.

Henry Robinson, 245 Rockingham St, 1855–1858.

RODGERS   Joseph Rodgers & Co, 33-35 Howard St, 1879–1886.

Joseph Rodgers & Sons, 6-7 Norfolk St, 29 Eyre St and Pond Hill, 1860–1970. The firm was founded in 1682 and became 'Ltd' in 1872. They were famous for their cutlery and were suppliers to Queen Victoria. Electroplating began in 1860. The trade names 'RODGERSLITE' and 'RODGERSINE' are sometimes encountered on cutlery. Mark 595 is an actual mark seen on a 1 pint water jug.

RODLEY   Thomas Heathcote Rodley, 63 West St, 1867–1872.

ROUND   Edward Round, 3 Broom Close, London Rd, 1853–1855.

Edwin Round & Son, 36 Holly St and Orchard Lane, 1872–1881. They became 'Ltd' in 1878. Edwin Round was previously a managing director of John Round & Son for 25 years.

*	1897–1901		591
C S	1863–1886	ROBINSON SHEFFIELD	592
*	1855–1858		593
C	1879–1886		594
* B C S	1860–1970	✳︎✝ JOSEPH RODGERS & SONS SHEFFIELD E.P.B.M X 263 2	595
*	1867–1872		596
*	1853–1855		597
*	1872–1881		598

ROUND
(continued)

John Round, Tudor Works, 6-13 Tudor St, 1847–1862. Became '& Son' in 1863.

John Round & Son, Tudor Works, 6-13 Tudor St, 1863–1930; Arundel Plate Works, 32-34 Eyre St, 1872–1885; Tudor Works, Pond Hill, 1930–1957. They became 'Ltd' in 1872. A previous electroplater, Joseph Ridge, was a manager between 1890-1915. The tradenames 'BENARES, KENDULAM & VALARIUM' are often encountered on cutlery. Mark 600 is an actual mark seen on a spoon. Mark 601 is an actual base mark seen on a condiment stand.

ROWAN

Henry Rowan, Jessop St, 1855–1857; 92 Wellington St, 1858–1863.

Joseph Rowan (Mustard & Pepper Tops), Court 1, 21-24 West Street Lane, 1872–1904. Became '& Son' in 1904.

Joseph Rowan & Son, 1 Devonshire Lane, 1904–1910.

Samuel Rowan, Orchard Works, Orchard Lane, 1878–1881.

RUSSELL

Russell & Travis, 76 Eyre St, 1861–1863. Prior to this Samuel Russell traded alone and continued to do so after the partnership dissolved. G Travis went on to form his own firm.

* B C S	1847–1862		599
* B C S	1863–1897		600
	1872–1957	 E PNS	601
*	1855–1863		602
*	1872-1904		603
*	1904–1910		604
*	1878–1881		605
* B	1861–1863		606

RUSSELL
(continued)

Samuel Russell, 12 Sheaf Gardens, 1859–1861. Formerly of Buxton & Russell, he went on to form Russell & Travis.

Samuel Russell, 20 Ellis St, 1864–1891. Formerly of Russell & Travis.

RUTHERFORD

William Rutherford, 28 Norfolk Rd, 1853–1855.

RYALLS

John Ryalls & Sons, Brunswick Works, 164-168 Eldon St, 1889–1914. Began electroplating in 1904.

RYLANDS

Rylands Electroplating Co. Ltd, 68-72 Eyre St, 1876–1930. William Ryland was previously a plater to the trade but formed and became Managing Director of this firm in 1876. Records indicate that they returned to plating for the trade only in c1910. Mark 611 is an actual base mark seen on an entree dish.

SAMPSON

Sampson, Wish & Co., Denmark Works, 3 Paradise St, 1872–1877. George Wish went on to trade from Norfolk Lane.

SANDERSON

Sanderson & Cokeham, Sylvester Gardens, 1884–1886. John Sanderson trading alone from 1887.

Sanderson & Roe, 34-36 Holly St, 1890–1894. John Sanderson returned to sole trading from 1895.

* **B**	1859–1861		607
* **B**	1864–1891		608
*	1853–1855		609
* **C**	1904–1914		610
* **C**	1876–c1910		611
* **B**	1872–1877		612
C	1884–1886		613
* **C**	1890–1894		614

SANDERSON   Edmund Sanderson, Sitwell Rd, c1889.
(continued)

John Sanderson, 18 Arundel St, 1887–
1889; 34-36 Holly St, 1895–1900. Formed
the partnership of Sanderson & Roe
between 1890–1894.

John Sanderson & Son (1929) Ltd,
Trafalgar St, 1929–1935.

Joseph Sanderson, 116 Sellers St, c1889.

SANSOM   Sansom & Davenport, 114 Rockinghan
St, 1853–1856. Became Sansom &
Creswick in 1856.

SANT   Frederick Thomas Sant, Alpha Works,
144 Eldon St, 1905–1911.

SARJEANT   John Alfred Sarjeant, 19 Cambridge St,
1928–1934.

SAVAGE   W Savage & Co., 52 Pond St, 1863–1867.
They shared the premises with Flanagan
& Paramore.

W S Savage & Co., 173 Pond St, 1876–
1929. Electroplated for the trade only
from 1900.

SCHOFIELD   Henry Schofield,17 Coal Pit Lane, 1858–
1859.

SCHOLES   Ernest Scholes, 9 Westfield Terrace,
1921–1952.

*	c1889		615
* C	1887–1889 & 1895–1900		616 617
*	1929–1935		618
*	c1889		619
* S	1853–1856		620
*	1905–1911		621
*	1928–1934		622
* C	1863–1867		623
* C	1876–1900		624
*	1858–1859		625
*	1921–1952		626

SCOTT   Thomas A Scott, 124 Fitzwilliam St, 1918–1923.

SEARS   William John Sears, 59 Arundel St, 1894–1904; 88-92 Trafalgar St, 1905–1930.

SEASALL   Edward S Seasall, Court 7, Eldon St, 1922–1925.

SELLERS   John Sellers & Sons, 151 Arundel St, 1838–1922. Started electroplating c1889.

SENIOR   Senior & Farquharson, 117A Fitzwilliam St, 1926–1940. Senior was formerly of Paget & Senior.

SHARMAN   Sharman & Hydes, Cyprus Works, Fawcett St, 1878–1881. Edwin Sharman traded solely from 1882.

Edwin Sharman, Cyprus Works, Daisy Walk, 1882–1886. Formerly of Sharman & Hydes.

SHARRARD   Sharrard, Mosley & Co. Ltd, 70 Trafalgar St, 1905–1910. Mark 634 is an actual mark seen on various items of cutlery.

SHAW   Shaw & Fisher, Norfolk Place, 39-43 Suffolk Rd, 1830–1894. Started electroplating c1849.

Shaw & Hewett, 40–42 Campo Lane, 1858-1861. Richard Shaw traded solely from 1861.

*	1918–1923		627
*	1894–1930		628
*	1922–1925		629
* C	1889–1922		630
*	1926–1940		631
* B	1878–1881		632
* B	1882–1886		633
C	1905–1910		634
* B C	c1870–1894		635
*	1858–1861		636

SHA

SHAW
(continued)

George Shaw, 147-149 Allen St, 1829–1857. Began electroplating in 1855 and became '& Co' in 1858.

George Shaw & Co., 147-149 Allen St, 1858–1862

John Shaw, 77 Milton St, 1858–1860.

Richard Shaw, 40 Campo Lane, 1861–1863. Formerly of Shaw & Hewett.

SHEFFIELD

Sheffield Cutlery Co-operative Society Ltd, 33 Leicester St, c1894.

Sheffield Electroplate & Cutlery Co., Central Works, West St, 1921–1925.

Sheffield Goods Supply Co., 39 Leadmill Rd, 1891–1894.

Sheffield Nickel & Silver Plating Co. Ltd, Globe Works, Green Lane, 1877–1898. Mark 644 is an actual base mark seen on a teapot.

Sheffield Plate Manufacturing Co. Ltd, Gatefield Works, 48 Robert St, 1884–1885. Alfred R Ecroyd acquired the trademark in 1885.

SHELDON

W Sheldon & Son, 188 Solly St, 1912–1935. Mark 645A is an actual base mark seen on a teapot.

SHILLITO

E Shillito & Co., 60 Cambridge St, 1904–1906; 28A Eyre Lane, 1907–1918; 38 Matilda St, 1919–1925.

* **B**	1855–1857		637
* **B**	1858–1862		638
*	1858–1860		639
*	1861–1863		640
C	c1894		641
* **C**	1921–1925		642
*	1891–1894		643
*	1877–1898	S. S. P. Ltd E P N S SHEFFIELD 9009	644
* **C**	1884–1885		645
* **B**	1912–1935	4 **W. SHELDON & SON** **SHEFFIELD** **1846**	645A
*	1904–1925		646

SHIRTCLIFFE   Frederick Shirtcliffe, Havelock Works, 41 Leadmill St, c1872.

W G Shirtcliffe & Son, 69 Arundel St, 1921–1931 Mark 648 is an actual base mark seen on an entree dish c1925.

William R Shirtcliffe, 229 Rockingham St, 1872–1881. 10 Rockingham Lane, 1878–1881. Became '& Son' in 1882.

William R Shirtcliffe & Son, 229 Rockingham St, 1882–1886.

SIBRAY   Sibray, Hall & Co, Fitzwalter Works, 111-115 St. Mary's Rd, 1878–1918. Became 'Ltd' in 1897.

SINGLETON   Singleton & Co, 10 Bakers Hill, 1889–1892. They became Singleton & Priestman in 1893.

Singleton & Priestman, Pond Hill, 1893–1910. Mark 653 is an actual mark seen on various items of cutlery. Formerly traded as Singleton & Co.

SISSONS   William & George Sissons, 9 Eyre St, 1858–1881; 75-77 St. Mary's Rd, 1881–1891. Formerly traded as Smiths, Sissons & Co. Charles & Walter Sissons inherited the business in 1885. The firm ceased electroplating c1891, but continued to trade well into the twentieth century.

* C	c1872		647
*	1921–1931		648
* C	1872–1881		649
* C	1882–1886		650
*	1878–1918		651
C	1889–1892		652
C	1893–1910		653
* S	1858–1891		654
	1858–1885		655
	1885–1891		656

SKINNER

Albert Skinner, 9 Eyre St, 1888-1890
Became '& Co.' in 1891.

Albert Skinner & Co., 9 Eyre St, 1891–
1893; 217 Shoreham St, 1894–1897.

Skinner & Branson, 17 Sycamore St,
1855–1858. Formerly traded as Skinner,
Coulson & Branson. Thomas Skinner
traded alone from 1858.

Skinner, Coulson & Branson,
17 Sycamore St, 1853–1855. In 1855
Coulson formed Coulson & Co. and the
remaining partners continued trading as
Skinner & Branson.

Thomas Skinner, 6 Regent Terrace,
1858–1860; 29 Charlotte St, 1861–1862;
Eldon St, 1863–1864; Trafalgar Lane,
1865–1867.

SLATER

Slater Brothers, 94 Scotland St, 1884–
1888; Beehive Works, 159-165
Fitzwilliam St, 1889–1904; 105 Arundel
St, 1904–1911. Formerly traded as J Slater
& Son.

J Slater & Son, 117 Norfolk St; 1867;
5 Duke St, 1868–1875; 5 Matilda St,
1876–1883. Became Slater Brothers in
1884.

Slater, Son & Horton, 117 Norfolk St,
1860–1867. Became J Slater & Son in
1867. Horton was formerly in Stacey,
Henry & Horton.

*	1888–1890		657
*	1891–1897		658
* **B**	1855–1858		659
* **B**	1853–1855		660
* **B**	1858–1867		661
* **B** **C**	1884–1911	 VENTURE Y. NOT	662
* **C**	1867–1883		663
* **C**	1860–1867		664

SMALLWOOD   Thomas Smallwood, Woodbank Crescent, Meersbrook Bank, Norton, 1881–1883.

SMITH   Charles Smith, 61 Suffolk Rd, 1857–1872. Mark 666 is taken from *Silver* by Joel Langford.

Smith, Sissons & Co, Eyre St, 1848–1858. Formerly traded as Roberts, Smith & Co. They became W & G Sissons in 1858.

SOUTHERN   Southern & Richardson, Don Cutlery Works, Doncaster St, 1863–1890. Began electroplating c1872.

SPOONER   Spooner & Ellin, 27 Radford St, 1863–1870; 135 Scotland St, 1871–1881; Central Works, 74 Mary St, 1882–1894.

STACEY   Stacey & Henry, 50 South St, 1855–1857; Norfolk St, 1858–1860. Also traded as Stacey, Henry & Horton.

Stacey, Henry & Horton – *see* Stacey & Henry. Horton went on to form Slater, Son & Horton.

Stacey Brothers, Art Works, Rockingham St, 1889–1893; 164 Eldon St, 1894–1900; Bishop St, 1900–1904.

Edward Henry Stacey, 12 Tudor St, 1862–1870.

*	1881–1883		665
*	1857–1872		666
*	1848–1858		667
* C	c1872–1890		668
C	1863–1894		669
* S	1855–1860		670
* S	1855–1860		671
* C	1889–1904		672
C	1862–1870		673

STACEY (continued)	E Stacey & Sons, Britannia Place, 36-40 Garden St, 1857–1923; 18-20 Fitzwilliam St, 1924–1934. Ebenezer's firm was a successor to the famous firm of John Vickers (the inventor of Britannia metal). They were taken over by Hodges Brothers in 1923. Mark 674 is an actual base mark seen on a loving cup.

G H Stacey & Co, Exchange Works, West St, 1872–1878. |
| **STANIFORTH** | Arthur Staniforth, Union Lane, 1923–1929. |
| **STEPHENSON** | W Stephenson & Co, 68 Holly St, 1914–1918. |
| **STEVENSON** | Stevenson & Law, 25 Orchard Lane, 1894–1899; 103-105 Carver St, 1900–1910. Mark 678 is an actual mark seen on a spoon.

Job Stevenson, 57–62 Milton St, 1858–1861; 2 Edgeton St, 1861–1863; 37 Eldon St, 1863–1875; Fitzwilliam Lane, 1875–1888; 47 Eyre Lane, 1889.

R Stevenson & Co., 27-29 Carver St, 1894–1900. Mark 680 is an actual base mark seen on a stand. |
| **STOKES** | Stokes, Ayres & Co., 37 Eldon St, 1921–1923; 36 Matilda St, 1924–1933; 31 Earl St, 1934–1942. |

* **B** **C**	1857–1934	Ⓔ Ⓢ ⓐ Ⓢ	674
*	1872–1878		675
*	1923–1929		676
*	1914–1918		677
C	1894–1910	PLURO SILVER	678
*	1858–1889		679
*	1894–1900	R S & C⁰ 906	680
*	1921–1942		681

STOKES (continued)	Charles Stokes, Shoreham Works, 465 Shoreham St, 1878–1881. Became '& Son' in 1882. Charles Stokes & Son, 465 Shoreham St, 1882–1887.
STRATFORD	George Stratford, 144 Fitzwilliam St, 1858–1859. Henry Stratford, 92 Harwood St, 1878–1930, became 'Ltd' in 1900. William & Henry Stratford, 10 Surrey St, 1855–1857; 1 New Church St, 1858–1878. Henry continued to trade solely from 1878.
SURREY	Surrey Plate Co., Surrey Lane, 1921–1925.
SWIFT	Joseph Swift & Co., 111 Arundel St, 1872–1881; Clyde Works, 1657 Shoreham St, 1882–1897. Formerly traded as Fee & Swift.
TAYLOR	Elisha Taylor (Pints & Co.), 118 Highfield, George Lane, 1852–1872, started electroplating c1865.
THICKETT	Godfrey Thickett, 66 Chester St, 1859–1860. John Thickett, 8 Hermitage St, 1860–1864; 41 Arundel St, 1865–1872. Formerly of Booth & Thickett.

*	1878–1881		682
*	1882–1887		683
*	1858–1859		684
*	1878–1930		685
* S	1855–1878	W S H S	686
*	1921–1925		687
*	1872–1897		688
* C	1865–1872		689
*	1859–1860		690
*	1860–1872		691

THO

SHEFFIELD ELECTROPLATED WARES

THOMPSON
Thompson & Brown, Eyre Lane, 1844–1848. Mark 692 was registered for use on sterling silver wares. It is probable that they never made any electroplated wares.

A H Thompson, 10-16 Regent St, 1886–1911. The initials stand for Albert Henry.

E L Thompson, 22 Mary St, 1883–1886; Central Works, 98 West St, 1887–1909; 12 Wostenholm Rd, 1910–1914. The initials stand for Edward Landers.

James Thompson, 12 Norfolk Lane, 1863–1864; Soho Place, 65 Napier St, 1864–1878; 99 Napier St, 1879–1887.

Joseph Thompson, 185 South St Park, 1858–1859.

William Thompson, 19 Carver St, 1889–1891.

TIDMARSH
J & C Tidmarsh, Wheeldon St, 1904–1909.

TIMM
Frederick Ellis Timm & Co., 11 Hawley Croft, 1860–1863; 10 Regent St, 1864–1886; 9 Eyre Lane, 1887–1896; Surrey Lane, 1897–1910; 137-139 Arundel St, 1910–1918. Originally he traded solely out of Belfield St, c1858–1860, specialising in handles and cups. Mark 699 is taken from *Silver* by Joel Langford.

* S	1844–1848	T & B	692
*	1886–1911		693
* C	1883–1914		694
*	1863–1887		695
* B S	1858–1859		696
*	1889–1891		697
*	1904–1909		698
* C	1860–1918	F . E . T & Co	699

TIMM
(Continued)

Herbert Timm, 23 Orchard Lane, 1889–1893. Formerly of Roberts & Timm, he went on to form Jenkins & Timm in 1894.

TOFIELD

Alfred Francis Tofield, 113 Eldon St, 1884–1886. Teamed up with James Tofield in 1887.

A F & J Tofield, 113 Eldon St, 1887–1888; Wilsick Works, 127-131 St. Mary's Rd, 1889–1896; 23 Furnival St, 1897–1900.

TOLPUTT

H Tolputt & Co. Ltd, New London Works, Bridge St, 1918–1923.

TOOTHILL

Maria Toothill, 18 School Croft, c1862.

Robert Toothill, 20 Bower Spring, 1858–1859.

TOWNDROW

Towndrow Brothers, 137-139 South St Moor, 1862–1872, formerly of J S Towndrow. Specialised in measures. Mark 706 is taken from *Silver* by Joel Langford.

J S Towndrow, 137-139 South St Moor, 1860–1861. Became Towndrow Brothers in 1862.

TOWNROE

John Townroe & Sons, 130-138 West St, 1861–1962. They were electroplaters to the trade only before 1887 and after 1916. Mark 708 is an actual base mark seen on a teapot.

*	1889–1893		700
*	1884–1886		701
*	1887–1900		702
*	1918–1923		703
B	c1862		704
B **C**	1858–1859		705
*	1862–1872		706
*	1860–1861		707
* **B**	1887–1916	J T & S	708

TOWNSEND Francis John Townsend, Cambridge Works, 214-216 Solly St, 1878–1905.

TRAVIS George Travis & Co., Clarence Works, 69 Charles St, 1864–1867; 13 Bath St, 1867–1908. Formerly of Russell & Travis, became Travis, Wilson & Co. Ltd in 1908.

Travis, Wilson & Co. Ltd, Clarence Works, 13 Bath St, 1908–1967.

TRICKETT Walter Trickett, 58 Holly Lane, 1894–1897; 27 Trippet Lane, 1898–1910.

TURNER Turner, Ryalls & Co. Ltd, 10 St. Thomas St, 1916–1923.

Thomas Turner & Co., Suffolk Works, 1 Suffolk Rd,1867–1940. Began electroplating in 1883 and became 'Sheffield Ltd' in 1916. Mark 714 is an actual mark seen on a spoon.

Mark 714A is an acutal mark seen on cutlery.

TURTON John Turton, 23–24 Times Buildings, Bow St, 1876-1898. Became '& Co.' in 1898.

---

* B C	1878–1905		709
* B	1864–1908		710
* B	1908–1967		711
*	1894–1910		712
*	1916–1923		713
* C S	1883–1940		714
	1916–1940	**T.TURNER & Co LTD** *Pedigree Plate*	714A
*	1876–1898		715

TUR

SHEFFIELD ELECTROPLATED WARES

TURTON
(continued)

John Turton & Co., Kendal Works, 57 Arundel St, 1898–1916; 21-29 Carver St, 1917–1923. Became 'Ltd' in 1910. Mark 716 is an actual base mark seen on a hot water jug. Mark 717 is an actual mark seen on a registered spoon dated c1921. Mark 718 is an actual mark seen on a basket.

TYLER

John Tyler, New Brunswick St, 1836–1869. Started electroplating in 1861. His son William Tyler took over in 1870. Mark 719 is taken from *Pewter* by D L Scott.

William Tyler, 11-15 Brunswick Rd, 1870–1900. Became '& Sons' in 1901. Mark 720 is an actual mark seen on a spoon.

William Tyler & Sons, 11-15 Brunswick Rd, 1901–1929.

TYSALL

Richard Tysall, 113 Eyre St, 1863–1864 and 173 Eyre St,1873–1886. Between 1865–1872 he partnered with his brother Alfred.

196

*	1898–1909	[J] [T] [&] [C°] [S] o 55 o	716
	1898–1923	[J T] [S] [✖] [E P]	717
	1910–1923	[J T] [&] [C°] [L^D] [S] [E][P][N][S] 2 0 4 6	718
* B	1861–1869	I. TYLER SHEFFIELD	719
* B C	1870–1900	(W.T) (S) (★) (♦)	720
* B C	1901–1929		721
*	1863–1864 & 1873–1886		722 723

TYSALL
(continued)

Richard & Alfred Tysall, 19 Norfolk Lane, 1865–1872. They specialised in toast racks.

TYZACK

Tyzack & Rhodes, Rockingham Plate Works, Rockingham Lane, c1876.

Edward Tyzack, 80 Division St, 1867–1873. Formerly traded as Pryor & Tyzack.

Joseph Tyzack, New George St, 1858–1859. Formerly Pryor Tyzack & Co. in 1860.

Tyzack, Vincent & Co., Cadman Lane, Norfolk St, 1886–1888. Tyzack later joined Needham, Veall & Tyzack.

UNWIN

Unwin & Rodgers Ltd, Globe Works, Green Lane and 124 Rockingham St and Penistone Rd, 1864–c1900. They also traded under the names James Rodgers & Co., and John Walters & Co. from c1886.

VIENER

Samuel Viener, Wentworth Works, Andrew St, 1923–1934.

W & E Viener, 136 West St,1908–1914; 76 Bath St, 1915–1924. Became Viners Ltd in 1925.

Viners Ltd, 76 Bath St and Broom Hall St, 1925–1974. Their trademarks 'ALPHA' and the 'crown' were taken from the firm of Harrison Brothers & Howson which ceased electroplating c1909. As with many other firms, their production of electroplated wares declined drastically at the outset of World War II, never fully recovering thereafter.

*	1865–1872		724
*	c1876		725
*	1867–1873		726
*	1858–1859		727
*	1886–1888		728
C	1864–1900		729
	1886–1900		730
*	1923–1934		731
* B	1908–1924		732
* B	1925–1974		733

WALKER

Walker & Co, 106 Mary St, 1909–1913; 21 Cambridge St, 1914–1918; 91 Button Lane, 1919–1940. Became 'Sheffield Ltd' in 1924. Mark 734 is an actual mark seen on an entree dish.

Walker & Coulson, 1845–1852. Went on to form Walker & Hall, and Skinner, Coulson & Branson respectively.

Walker & Hall, Electro Works, 9-15 Howard St, 1852–1961 and also 18 Eyre St, from 1894. Before teaming up with Henry Hall, George Walker was partnered with Samuel Coulson. They became 'Ltd' in 1923. The tradenames 'PALACE SILVER' and 'SONARA SILVER' are associated with this firm. Mark 736 is an actual mark seen on a spoon. Marks 738 and 739 are probably only seen on sterling silver wares. The letters J E B in mark 739 refer to John E Bingham who ran the firm during the period. **Note** – that a pair of crossed flags were used during the 1930s. Mark 742 is an actual mark seen on a spoon. Mappin & Webb took over the firm later in the twentieth century.

* **B**	1909–1940	**W & Co** **VICEROY PLATE**	734
C	1845–1852		735
* **C** **S**	1852–1897		736
	1861–1890		737
	from 1862		738
	1868–1916		739
	1891–1909		740
	1910–1970		741

WALKER
(continued)

Walker, Knowles & Co., 55-57 Burgess St, 1836–1861. Originally an Old Sheffield Plater. They started electroplating in 1853. **Note** – They are also known to have traded as S Walker & Co. Mark 744 was probably only used on sterling silver wares.

WALKLAND

James Walkland & Co., 122-124 West Bar, 1865–1885. They plated for the trade only from 1873.

James Walkland & Sons, 173 Rockingham St, 1915–1924.

WALL

H S Wall & Co., 50 Solly St, 1927–1930; 136 West St, 1931–1940. Mark 747 is an actual mark seen on a spoon.

WARBURTON

Elizabeth Warburton, 116 South St, 1858–1859.

WARD

Thomas Ward & Sons Ltd, Wardonia Works, Countess Rd, 1928–1952.

WARRISS

George Warriss, 28 Norfolk Lane, 1864–1865; School of Art Works, 53 Arundel St, 1865–1871; 32 Howard St, 1872–1891; 19 Eyre St and 32 Hanover St, 1892–1905. Became '& Sons' in 1906.

George Warriss & Sons, 19 Eyre St, 1906–1935.

	1920–1940		742
* S	1853–1861		743
	1853–1861		744
* B	1865–1872		745
*	1915–1924		746
C	1927–1940		747
* B	1858–1859		748
*	1928–1952		749
* C S	1864–1905		750
* C	1906–1935		751

WATSON Watson & Gilliott, 25 Furnival St, 1897–1899; 26 Eyre Lane, 1900–1940. Mark 752 is the actual base mark seen on a muffin bowl.

William Watson, Darnall, 1858–1872. Specialised in measures.

WEBSTER William Webster & Son, 14 Sycamore St, 1864–1897.

WENTWORTH The Wentworth Plate Co. Ltd, 33 Andrew St, 1932–1952.

WESTBY John Westby, 20 Cambridge St, 1894–1911; 4 Times Buildings, Bow St, 1900–1908; 1&16 Times Buildings, Bow St, 1909–1911. He was succeeded by his son Joseph in 1900.

WHEATLEY Wheatley Brothers, Wheatsheaf Works, John St and Eclipse Works, New George St, 1889–1922. Became 'Ltd' in 1914.

WHITE White & Johnstone, 53 North St, 1858–1864; Argentine Works, 16 Burgess St, 1865–1866. Became White Henderson & Co. in 1866.

*	1897–1940	W & G S zm	752
		945	
*	1858–1872		753
C	1864–1897		754
*	1932–1952		755
*	1894–1911		756
C	1889–1922	STANDARTE	757
	1889–1922	WHEAT SHEAF	758
* C	1858–1866	W.W T.J	759

WHITE
(continued)

White Henderson & Co., Electro Works, 16 Burgess St, 1866–1878. Formerly traded as White & Johnstone. Became White, Sons & Co. in 1878.

George T White, Napier Joint & Shovel Works, Napier St, 1881–1883.

John White, 19 Pond St, 1855–1858.

Thomas White, 21 Westfield Terrace, 1872–1891. Mark 763 is an actual base seen on a small oval dish.

White, Sons & Co., Electro Works, 16 Burgess St, 1878–1885.

WHITEHEAD

Henry Cox Whitehead, 80 Bowden St, 1897–1900.

WHITELEY

James T Whiteley, 20 Cambridge St, 1903–1922.

WHITTAKER

George Henry Whittaker, Pool Square, Fargate, 1881–1885. Became '& Co' in 1886.

George Henry Whittaker & Co., 8 Westfield Terrace, 1886–1891; 1 Cavendish St and 17-21 Convent Walk, 1892–1908; Wheeldon St, 1909–1911.

WIGFALL

John Wigfall & Co., Auckland Works, 37 Eldon St, 1889–1911.

* C	1866–1878		760
*	1881–1883		761
*	1855–1858		762
*	1872–1891		763
* C	1878–1885		764
* B	1897–1900		765
*	1903–1922		766
* C	1881–1885		767
* C	1886–1911		768
*	1889–1911		769

WILDE

Henry Wilde, 97 William St, 1858–1859.

WILKINSON

Wilkinson & Co., Arundel Works, 2 Howard Lane, and 226 Brookhill, 1878–1904.

Wilkinson Brothers, 9 Eyre St, 1885–1899; Eclipse Works, Boston St, 1900–1914.

Frederick William Wilkinson, 79 Rockingham Lane, 1889–1891; 57 Trafalgar St, 1892–1894. Became I & F Wilkinson in 1894.

Henry Wilkinson, 167 South St Park, 1858–1859; Great Green Lane, 1860–1863; Arundel Works, 13 Eyre Lane, 1864–1884; 76 Eyre Lane, 1885–1891; 63-65 Division St, 1892–1894. Became Wilkinson, Roberts & Co. in 1894. Henry Wilkinson began trading in 1828 producing Old Sheffield Plate.

Henry Wilkinson & Co., 20 Norfolk St, 1828–1871; 38 Norfolk St, 1872–1894. Started off producing Old Sheffield Plate and was the second firm in Sheffield to receive a licence to electroplate which it began in 1843. Became 'Ltd' in 1872. Mark 775 is the actual top mark on a condiment stand. Mark 776 is an actual mark seen on various items of cutlery. The trade name 'SILBA' is often encountered on cutlery. Mark 777 is the actual base mark to a cup.

*	1858–1859	770
*	1878–1904	771
* B	1885–1914	772
*	1889–1894	773
* B	1858–1894	774
* B C S	1843–1871	775
	1872–1894	776
	1872–1894	777

WILKINSON
(continued)

Henry D Wilkinson, 5 Union Lane, 1847–1859. The premises were taken over by Charles Anderton in 1860.

I & F Wilkinson, 57 Trafalgar St, 1894–1900. Formerly traded as F W Wilkinson.

Robert Wilkinson, Court 1, Norfolk Lane, 1858–1864.

Wilkinson, Roberts & Co., 63-65 Division St, 1894–1899; 226 Brookhill, 1900–1904. Formerly traded as Henry Wilkinson. Mark 781 is an actual mark seen on a spoon.

Thomas Wilkinson, Kenyon Alley, 223 Allen St and 95 New Edward St, 1867–1881.

WILLIAMS

Williams & Brooke, 2 Howard Lane, 1892–1898. Formerly traded as William Williams & Co.

Henry B Williams, Arundel Buildings, 57-59 Arundel St, 1897–1910.

William Williams & Co., 2 Howard Lane, 1886–1891. Became Williams & Brooke in 1892. Mark 785 is the actual base mark seen on a small sweetmeat basket.

WILLIAMSON

J Williamson & Sons, Napier St, 1884–1886.

WILLIS

George Willis & Co., 19 Carver St, 1921–1929.

*	1847–1859		778
*	1894–1900		779
*	1858–1864		780
* **C**	1894–1904		781
* **B**	1867–1881		782
*	1892–1898		783
*	1897–1910		784
*	1886–1891	W . W & Co	785
*	1884–1886		786
*	1921–1929		787

WILLIS
(continued)

Mark Willis, Exchange Works, 56 Fargate, 1872–1881; Tudor Place, 1882–1885. Became '& Son' in 1886. Mark 788 is an actual mark seen on a spoon.

Mark Willis & Son, Exchange Works, 207 Rockingham St, 1886–1918. Became 'Ltd' in 1904.

WILSON

Wilson & Davis, 41 Norfolk St and 19-21 Sycamore St, 1872–1881. Traded as Frederick Wilson & Co. from 1882. Mark 790 and 791 are both taken from *Silver* by Joel Langford.

Wilson Brothers, 14 New Church St, 1889–1891.

Frederick Wilson & Co., Hatton Works, 32 Eyre St, 1882–1887; 9-13 Cavendish St, 1888–1910. Formerly Wilson & Davis.

S Wilson, 94 Wellington St, 1865–1867. Formerly Methley & Wilson.

Thomas Wilson 157 Rockingham St, 1889–1890; 115 Milton St, 1891–1904; 173-175 Granville St, 1905–1910.

WING

George Wing, 10-12 Sycamore St, 1894–1909.

Samuel Sims Wing, 145 Eldon St, 1894–1896. Became S S Wing & Co. in 1897.

S S Wing & Co., 117 Eldon St, 1889–1899; 70 Trafalgar St, 1900–1910. Became 'Ltd' in 1900.

* C	1872–1885		788
* C	1886–1918		789
*	1872–1881		790
	1872–1881		791
*	1889–1891		792
* B	1882–1910		793
*	1865–1867		794
C	1889–1910		795
C	1894–1909		796
*	1894–1896		797
C	1889–1910		798

WINGFIELD Wingfield, Rowbotham & Co., Suffolk Rd and 82 Tenter St, 1889–1929. Also traded as Wade, Wingfield & Rowbotham.

Thomas Wingfield, 188 Rockingham St, 1922–1924.

W T Wingfield & Co., 148 Eyre St, 1905–1909. Mark 802 is an actual mark seen on a spoon.

WISH George Wish, Denmark Works, Norfolk Lane, 1878–1885; 16 Burgess St, 1886–1934. Formerly a partner in Sampson, Wish & Co. Became 'Ltd' in 1909. Mark 803 is the actual base mark seen on a water jug.

WITHEFORD William Arthur Witheford, Court 5, Brittain St, 1909–1944.

WOLSTENHOLME Wolstenholme & Biggin, Matilda Works, 117 Matilda St, 1876–1881. Formerly Wolstenholme, Maclaurin & Co. The site was taken over by George Maclaurin & Son in 1881, after which Henry Biggin traded from Arundel St.

J Wolstenholme, 10 Broad St Park, 1824–1839; 31 Broad St Park, 1840–1857 started electroplating in 1850. Joseph retired in 1857 and his son, W F Wolstenholme took over the firm.

* **B** **C**	1889–1929	*Trade Mark*	799
	1889–1929	WADE, WINGFIELD, AND ROWBOTHAM.	800
*	1922–1924		801
* **C**	1905–1909	WINGFIELDS AUSTRAL	802
* **B**	1878–1934	GW S E P B M 1 0 3 0 1	803
*	1909–1944		804
* **B**	1876–1881		805
* **B**	1850–1857	J . W	806

WOLSTENHOLME
(continued)

Wolstenholme, Maclaurin & Co., Matilda Works, 117 Matilda St, 1871-1875. A partnership formed between W F Wolstenholme and James Maclaurin & Sons. They became Wolstenholme & Biggin in 1876.

W F Wolstenholme, 31 Broad St, Park, 1858-1859; 43 Broad St, Park, 1860; Joiner Lane, 1861-1862; Stanley Lane Wickes, 1863-1870. The latter years were spent plating for the trade only. He went on to form Wolstenholme, Maclaurin & Co.

Wilfred Wolstenholme & Son, Ecclesall Works, 144 Rockingham Lane, 1882–1894. Wilfred was formerly in Wolstenholme & Biggin.

WOOD

Frank Wood, Helm Works, 41 Arundel St, 1898-1922.

WOODCOCK

Woodcock & Hardy, Eldon Place, 145 Eldon St, 1881-1897. Formerly Ridge, Woodcock & Hardy.

Thomas Woodcock & Sons, 43 Suffolk Rd, 1908–1929; 90 Eyre Lane, 1930–1957.

WORTH

B Worth & Sons, 195 Arundel St, 1900–1952.

* B	1871–1875		807
* B C	1858–1870	W . F . W	808
* B C	1882–1894		809
C	1898–1922		810
* B	1881–1897		811
* B	1908–1957		812
* C	1900–1952		813

WOSTENHOLM   Wostenholm & Co., Globe Works, Carver St, 1914–1918.

George Wostenholm & Son Ltd, Washington Works, Wellington St, c1880s.

WRIGHT   Wright & Co., Albert Works, Norfolk St, 1894–1900.

L J Wright & Co., 11 Priory Rd, 1905–1910.

Samuel Wright, 50 Solly St, 1905–1910.

YUDELMANN   Israel Yudelmann, 5-7 Westfield Terrace, 1905–1914; 32 Westfield Terrace, 1915–1925.

UNKNOWN   ?
Mark 820 is an actual mark seen on a teapot.

?
Marks 821 and 822 were both seen on cutlery. **Note** – the cross keys trademark prior to 1894 was used by Henry Wilkinson & Co. (*see* Mark 775).

UNKNOWN

*	1914–1918		814
* C	c1880s		815

*	1894–1900		816
*	1905–1910		817
*	1905–1910		818
*	1905–1925		819
*	?		820
C	c1894–?		821
	?		822

Appendix

NAME	TYPICAL MARKS
Daniel & Arter, Birmingham.	 ALUMINIUM, ARGENLINE, BENGAL, BRAZILIAN, BURMAROID, INDIAN, JAPANESE, LAXLEY, NEVADA SILVER.
Elkington & Co., Newall Street, Birmingham. **Note** – Crown in shield omitted from 1898.	 1865–1897 ELKINGTON & Co.
Joseph Gilbert, Sun Works, Ryland St, Birmingham.	 ALMADA ARGENTINA SILVER
Gotscher & Co., Birmingham.	  1745

Hukin & Heath, Birmingham.

William Page & Co.,
Birmingham.

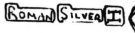

ASRISTA   . BOLIVIAN
ROMAN   SILVERITE SILVER

Potosi, The Company,
Birmingham.

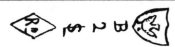

POTOSI SILVER

T Wilkinson & Sons,
Birmingham.

1 1 5

3 6 3 0

John Yates & Sons,
56 Pritchett St, Birmingham.

SILVER ASH, SILVERN
VIRGINIAN SILVER.

Bibliography

Silver, 1991, Joel Langford.

A Guide to Collecting Silver, 1980, Elizabeth De Castres.

Pewter Wares from Sheffield, 1980, Jack L. Scott.

Spinning Wheel Magazine (March, April and May), 1973,
   Jack L. Scott.

Silver, 1982, Judith Banister.

Renovating Silver, Pewter and Brass, 1980, Hamish Bowie.

Victorian Electroplate, 1971, Shirley Bury.

The Antique Buyers' Handbook, 1993, Peter Cook.

Silver and Sheffield Plate Marks, 1993, John Bly.

History of Old Sheffield Plate, 1968 (reprint),
   Frederick Bradbury.